PRASE FOR *

"With a mature Christian perspective and years of personal experience, Bernie Schock has given to parents of kids in sports a much-needed guide. He clearly explains the many benefits of involving our children in athletics, while, at the same time, insightfully dealing with the dangers and abuses. I know of no other book that is so helpful, practical, and needed as this one. All parents of kids and teenagers who are engaged in the world of competitive athletics should read this."

—Dr. Joseph Dillow and Linda Dillow

"As sports continue to occupy an increasingly prominent place in family life, many parents think only about their child's performance on the field. But as Bernie Schock points out, they could be missing the opportunity to use the short-term experience of organized sports to prepare them for the rest of their lives. I found myself nodding my head in agreement with many of the insights in his book. For parents who want their kids to get more out of hard organized sports than a home run, goal, or 300-yard drive, this book can serve as an indispensable guide."

—Tom Lehman, professional golfer

"This book is a 'must-read' for parents involved in youth sports and for those who aspire to be called 'coach.' Bernie Schock's experience, both as an athlete and as the parent of three competitive boys, gives great insight into the sports-crazed world we live in and captures the essence of what sports can be and should be all about."

—Brian Hansen, former NFL punter, South Dakota Fellowship of Christian Athletes (FCA) State Director

"The Bible frequently uses athletic metaphors to illustrate spiritual truths. Just as an athlete must strive to improve each day, God wants us to also strive to achieve a more intimate relationship with Him, and a more meaningful Christian walk on a day-to-day basis. *Raising Champions* is a book that beautifully combines athletic and coaching principles with sound Biblical teaching, and offers coaches, sports fans, parents of young athletes, and disciples of Christ a formula for success. Former Dallas Cowboy coach and NFL legend Tom Landry once said, "A man's quality is measured in direct proportion to his commitment to excellence." Bernie Schock is a man committed to excellence. He is man who 'walks his talk' when it comes to faith issues, and has an undeniable desire to glorify God in every endeavor he has ever undertaken. Knowing Bernie like I do, I can promise you that his hope for *Raising Champions* will be that the book serves as an important tool to challenge its readers to be strengthened in their own personal Christian journey. My good friend Irma Beekman, a counselor at a Christian school in Minnesota, once said, "A drop of ink can make thousands think." I'm glad that Bernie Schock has taken time to share with all of us who love sports and young people more drops of ink that have the capability to bring about positive changes and solid spiritual direction for each of our lives. I pray this book will give you strength and direction for today and hope for tomorrow. Congratulations, Bernie, on another winner!"

—Rick Nielsen, President and Founder, Blueprint For Life, Inc.

Raising Champions

Raising Champions

Helping Your Child Grow Through Sports

Bernie Schock

Trade paperback: ISBN: 978-1-939447-52-4
E-book: ISBN: 978-1-939447-53-1

Printed in the United States of America

Dedication

*To my three sons, Nathan, Andrew, and Jered,
who are a continuing delight to me and whose
participation in sports broadened my
understanding of how the sportsworld
impacts children.*

TABLE OF CONTENTS

INTRODUCTION

"Youth sports are second only to school in the amount of interest, investment, and involvement of parents on behalf of their children."

—Bob Bigelow

"Youth sports are the primary way that children socialize and, increasingly, the only way they play outdoors."

—Regan McMahon

My childhood dream was to play basketball for the Washington High School varsity team. As a result, I practiced for an hour or two on most winter days on my driveway—even in sub-freezing weather. (My parents appreciated my devotion because it kept our driveway mostly free of snow and ice!) This dream was so deeply embedded in me that well into my thirties, I still literally dreamed about being a star on my high school team—though in those later years I was a middle-aged man trying to disguise himself as an eighteen-year-old!

My dream was nurtured by a weekly ritual during the high school basketball season. A younger cousin and I eagerly attended the Friday-night games in a small gym that was bursting with raucous fans. Our fervor heightened as the team charged onto the floor while the band blasted the school song. After warm-ups, each starter was introduced and wildly cheered. As the teams circled for the center jump, we were on our feet, clapping and stomping: "Go! Go! Go! Go!" The energy generated by the game often kept the two of us playing one-on-one basketball past midnight in the driveway.

As I became an adult and reflected on my childhood devotion to sports, I began a search to understand the impact and meaning of sports for me and other children in our culture. That search led me to write my first book, *Parents, Kids and Sports*, and has also produced this sequel.

But why is a second book needed? First, it is needed because kids' sports have grown dramatically. In fact, the changes in the past twenty-five years could be summed up in one word, *more:*

- More children are competing—nearly fifty percent more than twenty-five years ago.

- More girls compete—nearly a tenfold increase in high school participation between 1970 and 2000!

- More children start earlier.

- More kids focus on one sport year-round.

- More is demanded of these athletes—more practices, more games, more travel.

- More is demanded of their families—more money, more involvement, more expectations.

- More injuries occur. Since 1995, there has been a fourfold increase in emergency-room visits for young athletes!

The predictable result of this flood of "*more*" is that children's sports schedules often dictate family schedules. As Dr. William Doherty, director of family therapy at the University of Minnesota, quipped: "The cart and the horse have switched positions in the last two decades." This development has led author and journalist Regan McMahon to ask:

> *How did we get here? Why do seasons for different sports have to overlap? Why does everyone I know spend so much of their time in the car, shuttling kids to practices and games? .... Is this really the best version of childhood we can offer our kids? Or is everyone giving up too much? Too many weekends, too many summers. Too much family time. Too much down time. Too many meals together at home.*

Our style of parenting has become the "roadrunner approach." This book will try to show how families can regain their balance so that kids' sports again become a servant to kids' broader needs.

Secondly, this follow-up book is needed because, paradoxically, the fitness of our children has imploded as participation has exploded. Research has found that almost half of American teens are not vigorously active on a regular basis and obesity among grade-school children has tripled over the past three decades (6.5% to 19.6%). Such statistics led Bruce Svare to conclude that "the young people of our nation have become fitness failures." How did this happen? How can they be fitness failures when so many are competing? This book will explore this mystery and try to help parents increase the fitness of their kids.

Thirdly, this new book is needed because the greater sportsworld has grown extensively in size and influence. During the summer of 1956 I began a baseball love affair with the Milwaukee Braves. (I jilted them when they moved to Atlanta.) My Braves were trying to hold onto a slim lead—which they eventually lost—over the Reds and the Dodgers. My only source of sports information was our local newspaper. Every day I waited anxiously for the evening paper and raced to the sports section to check the standings. But a young fan today has access to a gush of sports news and information. He can watch the highlights of the previous day's games all day on ESPN or on Major League Baseball's own channels. He can log onto his favorite team's website and find an abundant supply of game highlights, statistics, news, and interviews. He can watch sports talk shows for opinions about a recent game or the games still to be played. And he can watch nearly every Major League game on cable television or even on his smartphone. I was lucky to see my Braves play three or four times on television during the whole regular season!

Exposure to this expanding world of sports is unavoidable—even for the unathletic child. A child can't silence his peers' adulation of sports heroes or temper his father's passion for NFL football or skip a school pep rally. But how are kids affected by all of this zeal? And how can Christian parents rear children in our sports-saturated world who seek to be champions in God's world? I have written this book to help parents raise children who dream about being a star in God's kingdom.

Finally, I wanted to write another book about kids and sports because I have learned much from my experience over the past twenty years: I coached my youngest son's select soccer team for seven years; I coached all three of my boys' basketball teams at various times; I refereed youth soccer; and I watched my boys compete for their high school and college teams. In fact, at a time when I thought my dream of being a basketball star had died, I found that it was only dormant. Many of my old thoughts and feelings sprouted again when my sons began playing high school basketball!

This book and its predecessor are partly confessional. As I look back on my life, I understand that I had a lengthy affair with sports. This book isn't just about how to direct your child's heart. It is also about parents' hearts. We parents will never be able to help our kids until we understand why sports have such a powerful grip on many of us.

Conclusion

Travel writer Paul Theroux (*Dark Star Safari*) observed a group of
children at play one evening while waiting for a train in Tanzania:

> *A large gathering of children were kicking a soccer ball under
> the lights. It wasn't a proper game, but it was such hearty
> playing, with laughter and shouts, that it held my attention.
> Africa was full of skinny energetic children, and their game
> usually involved kicking a ball. These kids did not have a
> round rubber ball but rather a misshapen cloth ball stuffed
> with rags. The field was not flat and smooth—it was a
> succession of dirt piles and humps, very stony. The children
> played barefoot.*
>
> *Watching them play and call to each other on this hot
> night, I was impressed by their exertion and heartened by
> their high spirits. The playing field was a wasteland, and
> part of it lay in darkness. The children ran in and out of the
> shadows, screeching. The dark didn't matter, the bumpy field
> didn't matter, nor did the squashed ball. By any reckoning,
> these children were playing and laughing in one of the more
> desperate provinces of a semi-derelict country.*

The desire to play sports is universal. It can be a source of
great delight—but also great pain. In one national survey by
USA Today, 95% of parents expressed the idea that sports programs are important for kids' development. But in what ways?
What makes for good and bad experiences? I want to examine
children's sports through the lens of God's Truth, hopefully

providing a critical and loving analysis, so that sports can more frequently be a blessing to our children.

CHAPTER ONE

The Strengths of Children's Sports

"For every positive outcome in sports, there are possible negative outcomes. For example, sports can offer a child group membership or group exclusion, acceptance or rejection, a sense of accomplishment or a sense of failure, evidence of self-worth or a lack of evidence of self-worth."

—Dr. Terry Orlick, Sports Psychologist

No running back has dominated the NFL like Jim Brown did in the 1950s & 1960s. He won the rushing title for eight of the nine years of his career. He is still the only player to *average* over 100 yards per game rushing. He was voted into the NFL Pro Bowl every year. He accomplished all of this by the age of 29, when he retired, still in his prime. Brown believes that sports saved his life:

If I had never gone on to play at the professional level, I can safely say that the lessons I learned on the playing field in junior high and high school would have helped me through

life in any other field. I walked away from those experiences
knowing how to work hard, to concentrate. I knew how to
get up after I lost and how to cope with the fact that I wasn't
always going to win. These lessons helped me gain confidence.

I could easily fill several lengthy books with similar testimonies praising the role of sports in a child's life. Unfortunately, I could also fill several lengthy books with testimonies on the negative impact of sports on children. Why such diverse outcomes? To help your child's sports' stories be mostly positive, it is important to understand how sports can build up or tear down children. This chapter will focus on how sports boost the development of children.

Physical Development

> *"Johnny, would you please mow the lawn this afternoon?"*
> *"Dad, why do I always have to do it? Why don't you ask*
> *Mary once in a while?"*
> *"I do ask her to help. But I'm asking you to help this time."*
> *"But, Dad, you always make me do more."*

Ask a child to mow the lawn or scrub the tub, and he may complain like you've asked him to wash all the windows on the Empire State Building! But put him on a basketball court and he has boundless energy to play for hours. Children need from 30-60 minutes of vigorous, age-appropriate daily exercise. Sports are an easy way for children to meet that need.

Exercise enhances physical health by firming up our muscles. It also brings about positive changes in the cardiovascular system, reduces cholesterol and triglyceride levels in the blood, produces weight loss, reduces blood pressure readings, and reapportions body fat. Exercise also helps us sleep better, increases our energy, and reduces stress.

But exercise must continue if physical health is to be sustained. Sadly, the number of days per year that school-aged children exercise dropped by more than 10% during the 1990s. As a result, childhood obesity exploded, nearly doubling since the 1970s. Kids are obese, in part, because they drop out of sports—over 75% of them do so by the age of 15. However, if a child cultivates an interest in a lifetime sport, it often promotes an enduring commitment to exercise. When I practiced my basketball skills as a boy, I never dreamed that those skills would serve me for over 50 years! Pickup basketball is still a staple of my physical conditioning.

Why are today's children more sedentary? Because they spend an average of over six hours per day plugged into media—television, video games, the internet, smartphones, music, etc. (That's forty-two hours per week—equivalent to a full-time job!) Kids are watching Disney or texting their friends, but not playing soccer or riding their bikes. Children's health demands that we limit their use of media.

It is distressing that, as child obesity balloons, our schools are abandoning gym classes. By 2000 only 8% of elementary schools and 6% of middle and senior high schools offered daily physical education. Physical-education classes are being dropped to cut costs and focus on academics. If we want our children to be physically healthy, we can't depend on schools to make them that way.

Emotional Development

"Watch out, batter, batter! Here comes his high, hard one!"

"Hey, batter, this guy knocked a guy out last week!"

"Here it comes! Here it comes! Watch out! Duck!"

This was the atmosphere when my son, Jered, came to bat in a youth baseball game. His team was trailing by a run in their final at bat; there were two outs and the bases were loaded. On the first pitch, the pitcher lost control of his throw and beaned my son. After he fell to the ground, I raced onto the field and knelt by him. I stammered, "How ... how are you?" He answered: "I'm okay." Then he whispered: "It was better than striking out."

Sports expose children to a host of negative emotions: the fear of being hit by a baseball, worry about performance, discouragement from a loss, anger over a referee's decision. Sports can act as a classroom in which to learn how to handle those emotions. Fortunately, those troublesome emotions are usually washed away by other games and seasons. However, later in life, disappointments may not be so easily laundered. For example, the judgment of a man's boss may limit that man's lifelong opportunities. Sports allow children to experiment with emotions without suffering crushing consequences.

Furthermore, exercise can moderate some of these harmful emotions. A regular jogging program for emotionally disturbed boys made them more outgoing and emotionally stable than a control group of disturbed boys. Another study determined that a fifteen-minute walk was just as effective as a tranquilizer in reducing tension. Grade school teachers have long recognized that a fifteen-minute "tranquilizer" called "recess" is effective in reducing children's stress.

Anna Martin, a young woman who grew up in a broken, dysfunctional home, believes that basketball was God's gift to her. "To this day I know that God gave me the ability to play and love basketball so that I could have some sort of release in my life. It gave me an opportunity to get out of the house and get away from my family and release all of the emotions that were ripping me up inside." Though basketball wasn't a final remedy, it provided a temporary sanctuary during her troubled childhood.

Finally, sports may bolster children's emotional lives by communicating that it is okay to have fun. On many summer mornings during my youth I rode the bus across town to play sandlot baseball with my cousins. My mom was astonished at how early I would get up to play ball. We spent the cooler mornings playing baseball and the hot afternoons swimming. Reminiscing, I join writer Richard Lipsky as one of those "numberless American males who cling as long as life and common sense will let them to the days when a game of baseball could fill a whole hot afternoon so full that it would run over at the edges." Some of us have a tendency to work too hard, take life too seriously, and be too responsible. The Apostle Paul concluded his instructions about wealth by stating that God *richly provides us with everything for our enjoyment* (I Tim. 6:17). Money, sports, and other gifts are partly and graciously given for our *pleasure*.

Skill Development

Households through the centuries have echoed with children pleading, "Let me do it myself!" Kids want us to notice their achievements: "Look, Mommy, how fast I can run ... how far I can jump... how high I can climb!"

Mastering a skill is a special experience for all children. Consider this observation by author Gary Warner of a handicapped boy competing in the Special Olympics:

> *I saw a little boy stand for minutes, his eyes on the ground, sucking his finger, while two judges tried to convince him to make a try in the standing broad jump. Finally he made a token effort, hopping a few inches. He looked for approval and was applauded and hugged. He clasped his hands and laughed. And he jumped again. And again. And again. They could not get him to stop. Only a game of baseball among the angels could have been any happier.*

Maybe you've witnessed the toothy grin of a child who just learned how to ride a bike or one who finally achieved his first hit in a baseball game. Such accomplishments can help kids build the confidence that they need to tackle other challenges in life.

Sports skills are also important because athletic ability is a principal factor in gaining peer acceptance. When Christian kids are ostracized for their moral commitments, sports offer a healthy way to gain the acceptance of their peers. Psychologist Ronald Smith explains in his book *Kidsports* that sports also provide unique routes for some girls to gain positive peer approval:

> *The girl whose jeans and T-shirt can't be filled out nearly as well as her classmates' may very well be able to run faster, jump higher, and throw a ball better. In the past the very tall, late-maturing junior and senior high school girl often had less access to the mainstream of the most popular school activities. Women's basketball and volleyball have provided a welcome haven for these girls.*

Moral Development

Your modestly gifted team has toiled and tussled and somehow won enough games to play in a championship game. It is the final period, the game is tied, and you discover that your worst player has not played for the number of league-required minutes. What will you do? Is winning more important than moral excellence?

Coach Mike Slaughter's "once-in-a-lifetime" high school football team was 10-0 and headed to the state playoffs. But the week before their first game, sixteen of his starters (one was his son) were arrested for underage drinking; team rules called for their suspension. What would he do? Suspend the players or the team rules? Though he felt a deep "sense of hurt and betrayal," he never blinked. He suspended them all and played the game with second-teamers who lost 63-0. He believed that he had no other choice: "It boils down to accountability. It doesn't matter if they drank half a beer or a six-pack; they still broke the rules." The boys responded well. Though they weren't required to attend the game, they chose to dress in uniform and stand on the sidelines to cheer their replacements. Slaughter believed that their choice to attend the game "began the healing process. It gave the kids a chance to start facing up to what happened and go out like men."

Sports writer Heywood Hale Broun wrote that "Sports do not build character. They reveal it." When Coach Slaughter made the choice to suspend his players, he showed them that character is more important than championships.

Psychological Development

Christian psychologist Larry Crabb believes that, to be psychologically sound, people need both significance and security.

Significance

When our son Jered was twelve years old he competed in a championship soccer game that ended regulation in a tie. After a scoreless overtime period, the game was decided by a shootout—five penalty kicks for each team. My son's team won the shootout three to one and he scored one of those goals.

After the game I asked him, "Were you nervous?"

He responded, "Not really. The net looked so big, I didn't see how I could miss." Where did that confidence come from? It was based, in part, on previous soccer success.

Child development authority David Elkind explains in his book, *The Hurried Child,* that "childhood is the time when children establish either a firm sense of industry—that they can do a job and do it well—or an abiding sense of inferiority, a sense that whatever they undertake will end badly." Every child should feel uniquely good at something, whether it is playing a musical instrument, hitting a tennis ball, or drawing a picture. Success in sports can give children an "I-can-do-it" attitude toward other challenges, such as those at school, at work, in a marriage, or in a walk with God.

When I was a boy, my best friend and I played on a baseball team that was made up of boys who were cut by Little League teams. My minimally talented friend had two hitting goals that season. The first was to wrangle a walk as often as he could. He accomplished that with some frequency. The second was to make at least one hit during the season—that took longer. When he finally made contact and dribbled an infield hit, our bench erupted with joy! Success doesn't have to be measured by championships.

Security

Over the years I have had a growing sense of security in my marriage. With God's help, I have become more sensitive to

Cathy's moods—she no longer has to slam doors to get my attention! I communicate with her more frequently and with greater depth. I can occasionally admit my errors (though she doesn't think I do it often enough!). Even so, I still act like a punished puppy when criticized. I am about as neat as a junkyard. And I have a tendency to make opinions sound like demands. But even with such faults, I have no thought of her rejecting me. I feel secure because I know that she accepts me as I am.

To feel secure, a child must know that he is loved even when he falters ("I'm still loved even though I didn't make the team/I struck out with the bases loaded/I missed the crucial free throw"). A parent's gracious response to his child's "failures" (Hey, even Joe Mauer makes an out over 60% of the time!) will provide a secure base for his or her child to venture into the harsher adult world.

Social Development

A group of children gathers to play football. Last week the third-graders had bullied the second graders into age-divided teams. The obvious outcome made the younger group adamant: they refuse to play unless there is a more equitable division. They all are learning a lesson in fairness. A discussion of the rules follows. The bigger kids argue for tackle; the smaller ones plead for touch. This is a lesson in sensitivity to others. As the game progresses, conflicts arise: "I touched you!" "No you didn't!" "Yes I did!" The kids are learning a lesson in conflict resolution. A little later, one of the unskilled boys decides to quit. He is tired of hiking the ball on every play. But wait; he owns the football! His team quickly recognizes his untapped skills and lets him play quarterback for a few downs. The children are learning to be gracious to others.

Unfortunately, the above scene is quickly becoming fossilized because today's children seldom engage in freelance sports. When was the last time you saw a group of kids, without adults, playing a pick-up ball game? When adults organize the games, set the rules, negotiate the conflicts, and assess the skills, kids lose important developmental opportunities.

Research reported by Dr. Stuart Brown, the director of the National Institute for Play, has found that *none* of the murderers that he studied had engaged in normal rough-and-tumble play with other children. Brown surmises that when children play vigorously with each other, they develop knowledge of the limits of what is acceptable, what hurts, etc.

Intellectual Development

If I had trouble concentrating on my studies during my schooling, I would sometimes engage in strenuous exercise. It was more effective than caffeine when it came to keeping me alert. In fact, it was so effective that it created the opposite problem—insomnia!

Originally it was thought that crossword puzzles, reading, and other mind activities would stave off mental decline in the elderly. But recent studies have found that it isn't mental gymnastics, but rather gymnastics that keep us sharp. Research cited by Dr. Arthur Kramer in the Journal of Gerontology has found that "as little as three hours a week of brisk walking—no Stairmaster required—apparently increases blood flow to the brain and triggers biochemical changes that increase production of new brain neurons." Exercise tones our muscles and our brains.

Spiritual Development

Children's sporting experiences also provide great opportunities to grow spiritually. Though I will focus more directly on this issue in a later chapter, among the many potential spiritual benefits for athletes are learning how:

- to trust God for playing time and performance

- to love and encourage teammates

- to assess the relative importance of sports

- to accept the judgments of referees and coaches

Children who adopt God's perspective on their athletics will have a jumpstart on adult life.

Conclusion

As I have mentioned, I have been playing basketball for nearly six decades. This *habit* of exercise has served me well. It has helped me maintain my *physical health* (My waist measurement is the same as it was when I was 18!). My *mental health* has been bolstered by the praise ("Great pass!"). My *social health* has been fortified by the camaraderie.

Recently one of the younger guys I play with said, "You're over 60 years old! You sure have your shot down."

I responded: "I guess two hours of practice every day as a kid helped."

One of the other players jabbed, "Naw. You've just had a lot more years to perfect your shot!"

Sports can be a multifaceted blessing.

CHAPTER TWO

The Weaknesses of Children's Sports

"I'd root for Iraq against Duke."
— **North Carolina cheerleading coach**

It has been said that the church has too many unloving critics and too many uncritical lovers. Likewise, our criticism of sports often falls into one extreme or the other—reproaching sports harshly or praising sports naively. Loving critics can *improve* the opportunities for children in sports.

OVEREMPHASIS ON WINNING

The winning-is-everything attitude wounds all levels of sports. Flip Saunders coached the Detroit Pistons professional basketball team for three years beginning in 2005. During his tenure he won 70% of his games. He took his team to the conference finals (and lost) during each of those three years. His reward for such solid coaching? He was fired after the 2008 season. Management explained that "There are no sacred cows here. You lose that sacred-cow status when you lose three straight years like this." Lose? We're losers unless we win it all?! Ironically such a warped emphasis on winning seldom produces winners. Over the next four seasons the Pistons won less than 40% of their games and didn't once make the playoffs. Anyone want the "sacred cow" back?!

Some years ago, while watching a baseball game with my six-year-old son, he asked why the home team didn't bat in the bottom of the ninth inning. I explained that, since the home team was ahead, they would win the game whether they batted or not. He looked at me as if I had lost my mind and said, "So what?" He thought that the home team should feel cheated because they didn't get to bat as many times as the losing team. For him, playing was paramount; winning was secondary.

My son isn't alone; kids would rather play on a losing team than sit on the bench on a winning team. Surveys gathered by sports psychologist Ronald Smith indicate that kids participate in sports for the following reasons (listed in their order of importance):

1. **Have fun**
2. **Improve and learn new skills**
3. **Make and build friendships**
4. **Become physically fit**
5. **Win**

The boys I coached on my select soccer team certainly remember some of their big wins, but many of their fondest memories are about traveling, staying in hotels, playing "soccer tennis" (a game they invented and played on a tennis court), cooling off in swimming pools, hanging out with their friends, and staying up late. Winning was only one slice out of a large pie.

But when winning becomes the primary goal, there are a host of negative consequences for kids.

Abuse of People

A friend's six-year-old daughter was recruited to play on a softball team. At the beginning of the season, the coaches told the girls: "The pitcher is the most important player on the team." (Mistake #1: Elevating a player or a position. Kids should all feel significant.) Not surprisingly, my friend's daughter wanted to be one of those "most important" players, so she practiced her pitching. But when she had an opportunity to pitch during a scrimmage, she was so nervous that she didn't perform well. Even so, she was still scheduled to pitch an inning in their first game. When her inning came, she walked to the mound and started warming up. But her coach replaced her with another girl, explaining, "We need to win." Are you kidding me? Six year-olds?! (Mistake #2: Making winning the priority over the budding self-image of a young girl.) My friend explained that even though her daughter is a skilled hitter and a fast runner, the memory of her pitching failure still hurts. My friend also questioned her own choice: "I should have thought more about why coaches are recruiting first-grade girls!" (Mistake #3: Parents not investigating a coach or a sports program.)

Dr. Lyle Michaeli, in his practice in sports medicine at Children's Hospital in Boston, has encountered numerous mothers who abuse their gymnast daughters by practically starving them. They do this so that their bodies will remain immature and better suited to the sport. Thus, it is not surprising that some studies have indicated that college-age gymnasts are more prone to eating disorders than other female athletes.

Another type of abuse is the way in which elite athletes are coddled. Darcy Frey, in the book, *The Last Shot,* explains:

> *Today the best basketball teams play national schedules and Christmas tournaments in Vegas. Once a team is nationally ranked—USA Today runs a list, the "Super 25," of the best high school programs—the players can expect complimentary sneakers from the shoe companies looking to recruit future superstars and possible TV pitchmen, while the coaches receive annual stipends for keeping their players shod with the proper brand. One year Saint Raymond's, a parochial school in the Bronx, took its players to Hawaii, San Diego, and Anchorage.*

These young athletes are treated like gods until they graduate or their skills diminish.

The pressure to win also leads some athletes to abuse themselves by taking drugs like steroids. These performance-enhancing drugs help the body to metabolize the protein in food more efficiently and quickly, thus facilitating the production of muscle. They can also delay fatigue and create a feeling of euphoria. But steroids can also cause serious harm to young athletes, including infertility, delayed growth, high blood pressure, heart attacks, HIV/AIDS (from sharing needles), elevated aggression, delusions, and more.

We parents can protect our kids from drug abuse by not pressuring them to excel in sports. If it is truly "just a game," then kids will be less tempted to use these illegal drugs. Furthermore, sports organizations can help keep kids to stay clean. The state of Texas recognized a growing problem among high-school athletes and began to randomly test them. During the 2008-2009 school year, the state tested 45,193 student athletes, and only 19 of them tested positive for steroids.

Erosion of Morals

Try to think of a famous coach who doesn't win consistently. It is nearly impossible because, in the world of sports, winning "covers a multitude of sins and not winning is simply unforgivable." Winners are often perceived as good guys simply because they win—though their character might be appalling.

Willie Williams was an exceptional football player in high school. He had one small problem: he had been arrested 12 times—once on a recruiting trip! The University of Louisville's coach at that time, Bobby Petrino, still signed him to play for them. He later was kicked off UL's team when he was arrested (again!) on a drug charge. Though Mr. Williams may be one of the extreme cases, journalist Dan Le Batard contends in *ESPN The Magazine* that "you can't win at the highest levels of a sport as savage and cutthroat as college football without compromising some of your educational mission along the way."

Educational mission? At times, those words are a joke. One college's final exam in "Coaching Principles" had these "challenging" questions for the student athletes:

- How many halves are in a college basketball game?

- Diagram the half court line.

- How many goals are there on a basketball court?

- How many players can play at a time from one team?

Does it matter if I promise a young man a good education but place him in such mindless courses to ensure his eligibility? Does it matter if I lie about my child's age so that he can be successful among a younger group of athletes? Does it matter if a coach bends the rules so that his kids can win? Of course it matters! Listen to the testimony of one youth coach:

We have this must-play rule where every player is supposed to play a series every quarter. This coach worked out a scheme whereby he'd send the poor player, number 50, say, in with, say number 60. The woman who checks the subs—we call her the watchdog—checks off 50 and 60, coming in. Then as soon as 50 gets to the huddle he turns around and runs back off with the player 60 was sent in for. The watchdog wasn't asked to check who went out, only who went in. Number 50 never played.

Number 50 and the other players who witnessed this hoax were being abused. They were being taught that winning is more important than children—ouch!

We Christians in sports have also demonstrated an expedient ethic. At times, we have used the witness of big-name athletes without knowing the authenticity of their faith. We justify it by saying that it will attract more children to the gospel. But what happens when that athlete is arrested for a DUI? Or is seen cursing at a referee? Or later confesses that his faith was a fad? How does this affect the young athletes who heard his witness? Why not recruit a Christian athlete to speak who was cut from his college team? More athletes might identify with his struggles than with the all-star's success.

Damage to Identity

While attending a baseball tournament for preteen boys, I watched a game in which one of the teams was far superior. If I had coached the weaker team, I would have asked to see birth certificates! The weaker team's third baseman had to endure the brunt of the opponents' size and skill advantage as they easily pulled the pitches his way. Third base was literally a "hot box" and the young boy made several errors. The coach became so exasperated that he removed the boy in the middle of an inning. The dejected boy slumped to the dugout and buried his face in his glove. At the same time, the coach yelled a warning to his replacement: "Now, don't *you* let me down!"

A third consequence of an overemphasis on winning is that it can damage kids' identities. Had that baseball coach been more sensitive, he could have encouraged his young player: "Hey, Johnny, I know you're doing your best. Our problem is that the New York Yankees were directed to the wrong stadium!"

Research reported by sports psychologist Thomas Tutko, in his book *Winning is Everything and Other American Myths,* indicates that kids view winners as being better people than losers. Subjects in one study were asked to rate players according to their maturity, appearance, worth, and potency. The winners were rated consistently higher than the losers. Imagine what losing does to the identity of children when they believe that if they just had more character—not more skill— they would also be winners.

Losing the Fun

One year, our eldest son played on a championship soccer team. As the season progressed, the coaches scheduled extra practices and issued stern warnings about the next opponent. The parents attended the games with increasing consistency and enthusiasm, and the kids became more serious and determined. At the championship game, the intensity boiled over as the parents of the opposing teams exchanged heated words. What had happened? Somehow a shift had taken place—becoming champions became more important than having fun.

When NFL coach Bill Belichick began to win regularly, he met with Jimmy Johnson, the former coach of the Dallas Cowboys, to learn how to handle so much winning. Johnson talked about "the ordeal that came with success." Say what?! The ordeal?! We think that it is only the losers who aren't having fun. But Johnson said that the most difficult thing would be "the pressure that would come with winning. When you win, everyone wants more." Why do fans insist on more? Because winning does not satisfy the soul of a city or a school or a team or a player. God alone can quench our deepest thirsts—all other sources are *broken cisterns that cannot hold water* (Jer. 2:13).

Surveys indicate that 75% of child participants quit sports by the age of fifteen. And one-third of those who remain do so only to please a parent! Are kids running away from sports because we adults enthrone winning? If winning is king, kids who can't win won't compete.

OVERCONTROL BY ADULTS

Over the past few decades, children's play has become more heavily managed by adults. In kids' sports, adults determine the leagues, teams, schedules, practices, and rules. Though this has some advantages (e.g., vulnerable children can be protected), it also has substantial disadvantages.

Hindering Socialization

Let's replay the backyard football game from chapter one, but this time insert a typical adult. The first problem encountered was the selection of teams. The second-graders complain that they were coerced into playing the third-graders the week before. But now, with an adult present, the adult will squash the imbalance by selecting the teams himself. Remove lesson one on learning how to play fairly. Next, the children face the dilemma of whether to play tackle or touch. The adult, noting the difference in size and the presence of girls, would probably insist on touch. Remove lesson two on becoming sensitive to others' capabilities. And finally, when controversies arise ("I touched you!" "No you didn't!"), the adult will act as the referee. Remove lesson three on learning how to negotiate and compromise.

When our boys were young, Cathy and I recognized that we were intervening too much in their disputes. One day, our two older boys had a conflict while they were building with their blocks in the basement. When they couldn't solve it, they burst upstairs with a series of "I-had-it-firsts" and "No-you-didn'ts." I calmly told them that they would have to work it out themselves and sent them back downstairs. The argument quickly resumed, as did their pleading for intervention. I repeated that it was their responsibility to solve it, and if they didn't, the blocks would be put away. They groaned and complained, but returned to their play. A few minutes later, I noticed that it was quiet in the basement. I went down and asked them how they worked it out. They explained that they did some digging in the box of blocks and discovered a similar block that one of them could use. When adults are over involved in kids' play and games, kids lose opportunities to develop their social skills.

I have played pick-up basketball at our local YMCA for over four decades. In recent years the arguing has become so intense that the "Y" assigned a monitor to babysit our games. It is primarily the younger men who squabble the loudest and the longest. Their ability to compromise is minimal. I wonder ... Were their negotiating skills stunted because adults too often resolved the conflicts in their play? Are they also unskilled at resolving their conflicts at work, at home, with their friends? Children's games are a marvelous place for kids to build social skills that will serve them for a lifetime. We adults just need to get out of the way!

Hindering Self-Discipline

My eldest son played soccer for a Christian university. During the summer before his sophomore season, the coach sent out a very detailed letter about how the team should train physically (when and how to work out, what drills to practice, what to eat, etc.) and spiritually ("Read two chapters of Scripture each day and pray for at least twenty minutes for your teammates, coaches, and parents. Think for fifteen minutes each day on how you intend to be a better player, person, friend, and teammate.")

But do such detailed instructions cooperate with the long-term development of kids? One of the reasons our son was voted "Freshman of the Year" was that he had learned how to discipline himself. He arrived for team tryouts his freshman year having trained from one to two hours daily the preceding summer. If the coach's goal had been to help young men become independent, his summer letter might have counseled: "You need to be in shape when you arrive. I don't care how you do it; just do it. And don't take a break from your spiritual life either. I'll be praying that you spend time daily building your relationships with God and others."

Family therapist Peggy Wynne explains the serious consequences that may happen when adults do too much for kids: "If kids don't learn to entertain themselves, play by themselves, be creative in their own head, they're always looking for someone to stimulate them. Then when they get to be adolescents, they look for those quick fixes—drugs and alcohol—because that's a great way to get some kind of reaction to something, rather than learning how to make yourself happy doing something else." We parents need to stop choreographing our kids' lives, because it handicaps kids—and exhausts us!

OVERCOMPETIVENESS

Is the competitiveness in sports a problem? Not according to the late President Gerald Ford. He believed that "there are few things more important to a country's growth and well-being than competitive athletics." Many parents believe that through competition kids acquire skills that they will need to claim life's limited rewards. Not everyone can be class president. Not everyone can become a mayor. Not everyone will win a scholarship. But do competitive games help all children in such pursuits? Not always.

The Problem of Comparisons

Sports repeatedly expose children to comparisons, revealing who can throw farther, kick harder, run faster, score more, etc. And these comparisons can be especially damaging to the recurrent loser. As stated, childhood is the time to develop the confidence needed to do a job well. But when a child experiences negative comparisons again and again and again, it may lead him to feel incompetent or unworthy. This danger led sports psychologist Rainer Martens to ask in his book, *Joy and Sadness in Children's Sports*: "Have we not directed our sole attention to the winners and ignored the effects of competition upon losers who, as we have seen, constitute at least half the participants?" It may be that the extolling of competition has come from the winners.

Yet, you might ask, "Isn't sports just one area of a child's life? Can't losers in sports raise their confidence in other activities?" Some do, but many do not. The problem is that few other activities give as much recognition as athletics. In his book *Sports in America*, novelist James Michener wrote about his experience as an "A" student: "I can't recall a single instance in which any member of my community gave me any accolades for such accomplishment. In [my town] all that mattered was sports, and even today across America things are not much different."

A partial solution to the problem of comparisons is to measure a child's performance against her past performances: the time to run a race, the number of kicks in a soccer game, or the number of putts in a round of golf. If you keep individual statistics for your child, you will help her to feel good when she has improved her performance.

Even though there will always be comparative differences, it is the emphasis given to them that will mostly determine how children are affected. Thomas Tutko explains again:

> *Unless you give everyone the same kind of trophy, you're telling the loser, "You're different from the winner." But children know who the better ball players are. To give out trophies simply accentuates this difference. It makes the youngster who doesn't have talent feel even less capable, and it gives a distorted perspective to the child who gets the higher trophy.*

As children become older, though, they don't have to be crushed by these negative comparisons. They can use these appraisals to push themselves to become better athletes, or to recognize that their gifts lie elsewhere.

The Problem of Motivation

Jesus made it clear that life is a challenge. He told His disciples:

> *Enter through the narrow gate. For wide is the gate and broad is the road that leads to destruction, and many enter through it. But small is the gate and narrow the road that leads to life, and only a few find it. (Matthew 7:13, 14)*

The question, then, is not whether children need the motivation to tackle life's tough tasks, but whether sports *consistently* produce that motivation. As we have seen, repeated failure causes many kids to avoid a challenge. Educator and author Hollis Fait explains: "In the gym they may refuse to participate, become ill, complain of injury, or hide in line to avoid their turn. When pressured into making an attempt, they respond with a half-hearted effort that shows the others they aren't trying, for it's not so bad to fail if you don't really try."

Furthermore, even if competition encourages the pursuit of excellence, it is not the only way. In one study, students were asked to perform the same task in either a competitive or a cooperative group. The kids in the cooperative group not only produced a superior product, but also had a more favorable view of their group and a greater feeling of being liked.

The Problem of Selfishness

Competition incorporates a tendency toward self-concern. If you and I are striving for the same prize, I don't expect you to act generously on my behalf. In fact, if you become sympathetic while winning, you may ease up, allowing me to overtake you. It might then be said that you lack a "killer's instinct."

But don't team sports offset this selfish bent? Yes and no. Team sports offer greater, though not exclusive, opportunities for cooperation. A former college player spoke honestly about the joy that he felt when a teammate failed scholastically: "I remember figuring out on paper who my competition would be the next year and what their chances were of making it scholastically. I remember how elated I was when I found out a guy I was battling for second team had left school because of bad grades." Within a team there is rivalry to be the leading scorer, to gain playing time, and to receive recognition. It is difficult to be wholly concerned about the welfare of teammates when their success might limit yours.

Though self-interest in sport can never be eradicated, it can be mitigated. During the 2006 NCAA basketball tournament, George Mason University (GMU) made an unlikely run to the NCAA Final Four Championship, beating perennial powers Michigan State, North Carolina, and the University of Connecticut (UConn). After GMU's regional finals victory over Connecticut, UConn coach Jim Calhoun struck an admirable balance between the welfare of his team and that of his opponent: "I feel so good, through my own sadness, for Jim Larranaga" (George Mason's coach). Calhoun didn't let his own desire to win prevent him from rejoicing with the unlikely success of the opposing coach.

The Problem of Aggression

Some have theorized that sports act as a release for hostile feelings. One former President of the National Hockey League apparently believed that theory: "The spontaneous fight that breaks out as a result of frustration is an outlet. To eliminate that outlet is to bring about retaliation in more severe forms." What is he thinking—that players will wait outside the arena to blow away opponents with bazookas?! We should not condone hostility in sports at any level.

Though aggression is harmful, assertiveness is not. The goal for parents should not be to raise children with a "tread-on-me" attitude. These "nice" children become adults who "simply don't want to make waves [but] instead go along with the trend." But sometimes the waters need to be stirred; Jesus overturned tables in the temple. Writer Paul Coughlin in his book, *No More Jellyfish, Chickens, or Wimps,* has observed that "refusing to make waves is not an indicator of a life well-lived. Refusing to make waves is the state that precedes drowning."

Assertiveness can be taught. Whenever our boys had differences with a coach, we encouraged them to talk directly with him, rather than to complain to us or their teammates. Though at times we helped them to think through their complaints, they talked with their coaches on their own.

Conclusion

The greatest weakness of kids' sports may be the sheer *quantity* of them. Too many childhoods are being consumed by sports. Athletics was formerly one aspect of growing up, but now has become the primary focus for many children's lives. In a later chapter I will discuss how to balance athletics with the other experiences that children need to grow to maturity.

CHAPTER THREE
Guiding Your Child's Participation

"When it comes to making life good for our children, we are not quite sure where reasonable ends and ridiculous begins."

—Child Psychiatrist Alvin Rosenfeld & Nicole Wise

"To prevent even the tiniest mishap [for our kids], we believe we should act as stage managers responsible for all the production details: casting, costumes, scenery, music, script changes, and making sure no one ever misses a cue or flubs a line. And boy, does that keep us busy!"

—Developmental Psychologist Diane Ehrensaft

During the first year that I was old enough to play organized baseball, I tried out for a Little League team. Though I didn't make the team, I was blessed with a wonderful alternative. The city offered a league with four regional teams all coached by two brothers. We played games three mornings every week and there were *no* watching parents. In this low-pressure setting we boys learned how to play baseball. Years later, many of us became the stars of our high school teams.

Fast forward to 2013. I have a friend who referees summer-league basketball for high-schoolers. Though it is supposed to be a low-key experience with minimal coaching, my friend explains that there are twenty to thirty adults (mostly parents) at the games who relentlessly shout instructions to the players: "Block out on the rebound!" "Watch your passes!" "Don't give up the baseline!" "Come on—hustle out there!"

What has happened? Many parents today are tempted to have their "fingers in every mud pie their children make." They do this for reasons that feel solid and unselfish, desperately wanting what's best for their kids. But "guiding" is not a call to hectic, exhausting, non-stop involvement.

There are two dangers for the helping parent: over-involvement or under-involvement. Though, in the past, I mostly encouraged parents to *increase* their involvement in their children's lives, today I find a growing need to encourage overzealous parents to *decrease* their involvement. This chapter will focus on what are appropriate, and at times, inappropriate, ways to be involved in your child's athletic life.

PARENTS AS INTERPRETERS

When I was my son Andrew's soccer coach, I played him as a midfielder. Though he scored an occasional goal, I told him that his job was broader than that—he also had to think defensively. But his older brother, Nathan, was a scorer. After one game in which Nathan had scored two goals, he gave the family a very animated description of how he had scored. Near the end of his story, Andrew leaned over to me and whispered, "Dad, I'm not supposed to score goals, am I?"

I whispered back, "No, Andrew, your job is to take the ball from our opponents and feed it to our scorers." Andrew became content with not scoring, because success had been defined to match his talents and his role.

The ability to interpret life accurately is fundamental to maturity. People are not so much shaped by circumstances, as they are by their *interpretation* of those circumstances. When my middle son felt uneasy listening to his older brother's exploits, I helped him to understand his experience in the light of truth. When your child scores a winning goal or fouls out of a basketball game or strikes out with the bases loaded, she may need help with her perspective on those athletic highs and lows.

Interpreting Failure: The Success of Failure

When one of our sons was a junior in high school, he was playing behind a boy on his basketball team who wasn't nearly as talented as he was. (This wasn't just a parental prejudice! It was also the opinion of a local college coach.) After one of his games in which he played little, he grumbled, "I work hard, practice extra, play well when I'm in the game, but get little playing time. Other guys never practice, play just okay, and get lots of playing time. I'm not sure I want to play next year." Our dejected son needed help.

Initially, we reminded him that his extra practice had paid off; he was leading the team in field goal percentage. We also pointed out that his team had been playing weak teams and that he would have an opportunity to shine when they faced stiffer competition. Finally, we encouraged him to think about God's purpose in all of this. Was God teaching him how to be content "in all circumstances?" To love his teammates? To trust God for his playing time?

The following week, the boy our son was playing behind was injured and wouldn't play in the next game—a game against a difficult opponent. We asked several people to pray for our son. We prayed together as a family. The result? He played little and poorly. Did God answer our prayers? Definitely! As a result of his discouraging performance and season, he went to his closet and dug out information that he had received at a Fellowship of Christian Athletes camp about how God helps us in our adversity. Our son was learning how to connect with God in his pain.

As the season continued, our son had highs (e.g., a critical role in the district final win—ten points, four assists, no turnovers) and lows (e.g., little playing time during state tournament games). But he—and his parents—were learning again and again to put hope in God, not in the circumstances. *Why, my soul, are you downcast? Why so disturbed within me? Put your hope in God, for I will yet praise him.* (Psalms 42:5)

If the source of an athlete's happiness is praise or playing time or plaques, he will eventually experience a great deal of *un*happiness.

Parents, please note that losing can be a powerful instrument for growth in your kids. Our son's "failure" became the basis of his success. He grew in ways that would not have happened had he been a star on the court.

Interpreting Success: The Failure of Success

Don Simpson, a co-producer of the popular Tom Cruise movie *Top Gun,* said that he and his partner, Jerry Bruckheimer, "side with the winners; we aren't interested in the losers—they're boring to us." These filmmakers reflect the dominant cultural view that you are a hero if you win and a bum if you lose. (Research has found that boys, in particular, have a hard time feeling good about themselves when they lose.)

When the larger culture worships winners, many kids feel pressure to succeed. Psychologist Roni Cohen-Sandler, in her work with teen girls, has found that no matter what their age or social status or educational ability, "almost without exception they tell me that they feel stressed by pressures to excel." Many of them believe that to be successful they have to be extraordinary. With such a towering standard, many girls report being "totally stressed-out," "overwhelmed," and "completely exhausted." They "think that besides acing every subject, they must also star in their school plays, shine in music, excel athletically, be popular, and win awards." The path to success is dangerously steep for many kids.

Ryan Hall, the United States' top marathoner during the 2000s, was nearly a casualty of this pressure to excel. Hall set lofty goals for himself. But when his goal to make the 2004 Olympic Team became an obsession, it led to burnout. On some mornings he could barely climb out of bed. Hall explained: "There wasn't anything wrong with my body; I was just emotionally and spiritually wrecked." When he changed his goal to simply being faithful to God, he found freedom and greater success. He told God: "Whatever you want to do with it, do it. If you want to take me to the Olympics, great. If You don't, that's great, too." Running became a delight again because he had the "freedom to not have to achieve."

Like Ryan Hall, our son wanted to be successful in basketball. But he had to learn that, in God's world, he is successful when he is faithful: *It is required that those who have been given a trust must prove faithful.* (1 Cor. 4:2) He was successful when he practiced hard, when he refined his God-given skills, when he didn't grumble about his coach's decisions, and when he cheered his teammates— even the one playing ahead of him! His performance might not have looked significant in the team's season-ending statistics, but God keeps a different set of books!

Eventually kids need to be able to judge their own experience. Appropriate questions can help:

- "I heard your coach chew you out during the game. How did it make you feel? How would God want you to respond?"

- "Why do you think Tommy is so bossy? How do the other boys react to him?"

- "What do you do well? Not so well?"

Don't pressure them to come up with the *right* answer every time. Older children have to choose some *wrong* answers as they learn how to see life through God's eyes.

PARENTS AS ENCOURAGERS

The apostles gave Joseph the nickname "Barnabas," which means "son of encouragement." Because Barnabas was adept at building confidence and courage in others, God chose him to nurture some of the first Gentile converts, as well as the Apostle Paul. Barnabas was a man who saw potential and offered support while the potential was being reached. Our children need that same kind of encouragement.

Building Confidence Through Praise

The Apostle Paul's strategy to stimulate future growth was to build on past success: *We instructed you how to live in order to please God, as in fact you are living. Now, we ask you and urge you in the Lord Jesus to do this more and more.* (1 Thess. 4:9,10) They were traveling on the right path and he wanted them to continue on it.

Following Paul's model, a parent should praise what his child does well, even when there is much room for improvement. If your daughter is unaggressive in a basketball game, don't whine about her lack of intensity. Commend her for a rebound that she battled for and won. If your son made an error in a baseball game, praise one of his good plays: "You did a great job gauging the wind on that pop fly in the second inning. Not many fifth-graders could make that play!" Some parents withhold praise because they think that it would give their child a "big head." But most often, the braggart's self-praise is a vain attempt to meet his need for approval. If you don't praise him, he will praise himself.

Commending your child's successes, though, does not mean that you never discuss his failures. When your child moans over a subpar performance, don't falsely praise him by saying "Good job!" He knows better and will resent your good-willed lie. It might be better to simply say, "That wasn't one of your better efforts." And you might add later: "I think you're not improving because you seldom practice." Or if your child has a number of bad performances, he might need to hear "Tom, you're a better basketball player than a soccer player. Would you like to put more time into developing your basketball skills?" Be careful, though, as to *when* you offer criticism; directly after a game, his emotions may obstruct his hearing. Not even professional athletes like post-game interviews!

Hall-of-fame football coach Lou Holtz believes that *American Idol* testifies to the failure of some parents to speak truth to their children:

> *The less-than-skilled singers auditioning for American Idol*
> *is as staggering as it is sad. Simon Cowell, one of the judges*
> *on the show, has gained a reputation as being the "mean old*
> *bad guy" because he tells people the truth: some of them simply*
> *can't sing. The fact that they've never been told this for fear*

of hurting their feelings is a troubling commentary on what we value today.

When parents hand out "junk praise," it may impede children's ability to discern how God has gifted them. Your child needs help assessing his strengths and weaknesses so that he can discover God's design for his life.

Finally, we parents must not overpraise *athletic* achievement. Educator and coach Bruce Svare praised his father's values: "I am almost certain that my father was more proud of my academic accomplishments than he ever was of anything I did on the basketball court or football field." Think about it: Do you show (at least) as much interest in your child's academics as you do in her sports? Even when our sons were in college, we tried to maintain a balance during our visits; we not only watched their athletic contests, but we also attended some of their classes.

Building Confidence Through Practice

When my eldest son was a senior in high school, his performance on his basketball team had slipped as a result of injuries and inconsistent shooting. As his team was preparing for the season-ending playoffs, he asked me to help him practice his shooting. Over the next few days, I spent a couple of hours helping him. The practice paid off. In the district final, he had a solid game, scoring nine points in the first quarter as his team coasted to a fifteen-point win. Next in line was the regional final against the number-one team in the state; the winner would advance to the state tournament. Before that game I told my son that I thought that he would have another big game. The game started disastrously; three minutes into it he was benched with his second foul. Cathy and I had been praying with our son that if the season were to end there, it would end on a positive note for him and the team. When I saw him heading toward the bench, I sighed and prayed, "Okay, Lord, you know what is best."

But when my son entered the game again in the second quarter, he quickly made two baskets and a free throw. Both he and the team went on to have an outstanding game, even though they lost a squeaker to that #1 team. At one point in the second half of the game, after my son had made his third three pointer in a row, he looked over at me, smiled, and gave me a thumbs-up sign—thanking me for my help and my confidence in him. After the game, we thanked God that the season had ended well for him and the team.

As expected, kids who practice their skills are the ones who are the most accomplished athletes. All a child needs is someone who will play catch with him, rebound his basketball, retrieve batted balls, or transport him to the driving range. (Dads, practicing with your daughter can be a good way to find common ground and build your relationship with her.)

Should you ever prod your child to practice? Certainly. Don't you urge her to practice her music lessons? To work at her studies? But be careful:

- Keep age-appropriate expectations. A five year-old's interest may shift after one or two minutes. Let her quit.

- Don't use guilt to motivate ("I spend lots of money so you can play on this team. The least you can do is practice!")

- Give older children increasing responsibility for their training so that they learn *self*-discipline.

- Be sure that you are also urging him to be a good brother, a committed student, and a faithful child of God. Athletic skills will be relatively unimportant in his adult life.

- Check your motivation. Is your child's athletic life one last chance to be a star yourself?

This last issue, the temptation to live through our children's achievements, is particularly dangerous. Since we all harbor an enormous capacity for self-deception, it is important to search our motives. Ask your child or your spouse "Am I pushing too hard?" Examine how you respond to your child's performance. Are you thrilled when he wins? Despondent when he loses or plays poorly? Remember: Your kids don't exist to fill you up—that is God's job!

Building Confidence through Conditioning

Athletic trainers inform us that it takes six to eight weeks for a child to get into peak condition—about the length of a normal athletic season. So if your child doesn't begin conditioning his body before the season begins, he won't perform as well as he could.

Obviously, training must be age-specific. When our boys were preteens, the routines of our family included exercise. We biked, kicked soccer balls, swam, and threw frisbees. In one of our houses, we had a long basement room that we left mostly unfinished so that the boys had a place for their rambunctious winter games. In all of this, they were being subconsciously conditioned. Exercise was fun. (What ten year-old believes you when you tell him that running is good for him? It sounds like the plea to study so he can get into a good college!)

Younger children should have no more than three hard workouts per week because exercise mildly injures muscles. If kids alternate between exercise and rest, their muscle tissue will be strengthened. Some coaches conduct a rigorous practice the night before a game and then wonder why their team seems flat the next day. If you want to maximize your child's performance, an activity like a long bike ride might be avoided on game day.

As a child moves into the teen years, she may choose to develop a more serious and disciplined approach to her training. But she should seek the advice and guidance of a professional coach or trainer. The wrong training can damage health and performance.

Proper nutrition is also an important part of conditioning. Child athletes have unique nutritional needs; they need more food and water. The need for more food can be met with three meals plus a few healthy snacks each day. The need for more water can be met by being sure that competing athletes have plenty of liquids. If a child loses just 2% of his weight through perspiration, it can lead to cramping, heat exhaustion, and even heat stroke. Young kids are especially vulnerable because they don't sweat efficiently and can become easily overheated. During very hot weather, their games should be shortened or rescheduled. The goal of training isn't to create a star athlete but a lifelong athlete. The benefits of exercise are profound but short-lived. If you help your child develop a *habit of exercise*, it will serve him long after his last childhood game.

Building Confidence in Your Unathletic Child

A clumsy child may find a walk through the house as dangerous as a walk through a minefield! It may be even more risky for him to step onto a ball field where winners are praised and losers are ignored or berated. What can a parent do?

First, take great care in selecting a sport. Avoid programs that place a heavy emphasis on winning or don't give each child a generous opportunity to play.

Second, be realistic. Though he may never be a star, he can enjoy sports if you help him to set reasonable goals:

- Scoring one goal in a season

- Making 50% of his free throws

- Tackling two opponents

- Making a new friend

- Playing for a certain number of minutes

Third, note that extra practice is essential for the unathletic child. Since he doesn't have much natural talent, he will need to develop skills that will help him compete.

Finally, be careful about sibling comparison. Author Chap Clark's oldest son was an immediate success of the soccer field, scoring a goal in almost every game. Chap wanted to reward his son for his good play, so he took him for a post-game milkshake after any game in which he scored. But Chap never thought about how this ritual would be interpreted by his less-talented second son: "Somewhere near the end of his second year of soccer, I noticed a tear slip down his cheek as we drove by McDonald's: 'I guess I'll never get a milkshake, huh, Dad?'" Clark felt sick: "Even as I type this, I feel myself withering on the inside. With every fiber of my being I wanted the best for my boy and to be his fan and encourager. It simply never occurred to me that rewarding one son... would have such a painful impact on the other son."

PARENTS AS LISTENERS

Plato believed he could learn more about a person in an hour of play than in a year of conversation. Similarly, as you watch your child compete, you can "hear" an earful about how she is developing. How does she handle losing? What happens when the referee makes a bad call? How does she relate to her team-mates? Sports can be a mirror to her soul—if you learn her languages.

The Language of Injuries

It is early in the basketball game. Eight-year-old Bill twists his ankle and limps to the bench. A little later he returns to the game but soon collides with a bigger boy and, once again, shuffles to the bench. His frequent injuries are a pattern. Is he more prone to injuries than other boys? Dr. James Garrick believes that these undetectable injuries in athletes mean "one of two things: (a) we're not smart enough to find the injury or (b) they don't want to play." I believe that Bill didn't want to play. His mother offered a running and loud critique of his performance from the sidelines. Bill found safety on the bench.

The Language of Stress

Stress is normal in sports; a child may have difficulty sleeping or experience "butterflies" before a big game. But one study found that about 10% of athletes were under excessive stress— that is 2.5 million kids! How do you know if your child is overly stressed? He may show it in one of these ways:

- In his body — frequent headaches, sleepless nights, digestive problems

- In his performance — consistently underperforming

- In his attitude — "I'm no good. I want to quit."

- In his emotions — "I play with a bunch of losers!"

The stress that you see in your child's athletic life may not come exclusively from sports. One psychologist for girls has found that "pressure comes from everyone—parents, teachers, media, friends, boyfriends, coaches. Teachers may want you to focus more in their class. The media shows you stick-thin models.

Parents want you to do well in everything. Friends demand your attention. Coaches push you hard, wanting you to work hard and lose weight. Your boyfriend may want you to grow your hair." Thus, stress is only a signal. Your child may not enjoy her athletics until you deal with the underlying cause(s) of the stress.

Other Languages

Is your teen daughter losing weight? Have her periods become irregular? What does this say? Some girls believe that their athletic performance will improve if they lose weight. Often these ideas can be traced to their coaches, particularly in sports that place an emphasis on physical appearance (gymnastics, figure skating, diving, dance, etc.). But if they are in shape, losing weight will only decrease their strength. And if they continue to lose weight, it may interfere with their menstrual cycle (through a loss of estrogen) and eventually lead to eating disorders or even osteoporosis. These are serious issues. Get help for your daughter before the problem becomes severe.

The messages that our kids send aren't all negative. As I have said, when my eldest son was a junior in high school he was probably the second or third best player on the team, but was playing half or less of each game. But while I was frustrated, he remained mostly positive. Unlike his dad, he was developing into a young man who didn't get his life's meaning from athletics. I could only pray, "Thank you, Lord, for his growing maturity."

Conclusion

I began this chapter by expressing concern that some parents
are too involved in their children's sports. How do you know
if you are one of those parents? You are probably doing too
much if:

- You don't have time for a date night with your
  spouse.

- One of your other children resents the time that
  you spend with his sibling's sports.

- You don't have time to join a Bible study or take
  a family vacation.

- You never miss one of your child's games.

Making your child *the* central focus of your life can be disastrous for your child. She may come to feel that she should be
the central focus of *everyone's* attention! Marriage counselors
hear this attitude repeatedly: "*I'm* not getting *my* needs met."
Your child needs your guidance, but not your hovering devotion.

CHAPTER FOUR

Choosing a Sport

"Our culture is not lifetime-sport-oriented."
**— Dr. Bruce Svare, Director of the National
Institute for Sports Reform**

Bill Veeck, the former owner of the Chicago White Sox, once joked, "Baseball is the only game left for people. To play basketball now, you have to be seven-foot-six. To play football you have to be the same width." A recent survey reported in *USA Today* found that parents believe that basketball (39%) is the best sport for kids. Baseball followed closely (36%), and then soccer (15%). But what sport is best for *your* child? A good selection will enhance a child's experience.

WHEN: CHILDREN'S READINESS FOR SPORTS

When I was a boy, I had no opportunity to participate in organized sports until I reached the age of nine. Today, many children begin at the age of three or four, and some begin even younger. Is that wise? When are children ready for organized competition?

Family Needs

At one exhausted point, when our three boys were playing both spring and fall soccer, I estimated that their yearly commitments totaled more than 100 games and practices! And they were also playing other sports. Dr. William Doherty, wonders, "How did children's sports come to consume so much of family life?"

Before you register your child for any organized sport, consider the larger picture: How will this affect the whole family? Christian psychologist John Rosemond believes that "no other relationship or enterprise of any sort should come before [the parents'] relationship with each other." In many homes, couples build their lives around their kids and neglect their marriages. That is why the second highest divorce rate is found in the years immediately *after* children leave the nest. As our boys were growing up, Cathy and I maintained a weekly date night, we vacationed without our kids, and we didn't let their athletic schedule trump all other commitments. Did we miss some of their contests? Of course. But we were committed to putting God and each other ahead of the boys' athletic commitments.

Sports choices should also consider the needs of non-participating siblings. How will a brother feel if he is either dragged along or forced to stay with relatives while his sister travels ten to fifteen weekends a year to play soccer? No child should be required to do that year after year.

A Child's Needs

When considering a child's participation in sports, it is important to focus on the genuine needs of growing children.

Time for Connection

I rush in the front door from work and find my son enjoying a cookie and a glass of milk. I pull up a chair and announce, "Hey, I don't have much time; I've got to leave for a church meeting in five minutes. But let's talk. You tell me all about your hopes and dreams and problems and I'll share with you some wisdom to help you grow up to be a godly man. But talk fast; we only have four minutes left." Ridiculous? Obviously. Kids desperately need to bond with their parents, but it won't happen in five-minute bursts, or while sitting on the sidelines of their athletic contests. It can happen, though, at mealtime or bedtime, on family vacations, or while working together on a household project. When our boys were young, we tucked them in bed with the invitation to "talk about the day." Talking about the highlights of the day was an unhurried, satisfying way to end our boys' day and helped us connect in significant ways.

Encouraging Diversity

Family vacations at Lake Okoboji were the highpoint of my childhood summers. We swam and fished; we played ping-pong and pinball; we ate gobs of sweet corn and peaches; and we even competed in a talent show! My baseball coach didn't like it, but he understood that family vacations came first. But during the last two decades of the twentieth century, family vacations declined by nearly thity percent. And one of the main deterrents? Children's sports.

When I was in high school, I played on a city-league baseball team and an all-star team. I played a combined total of thirty to thirty-five games each summer. But a high-school player today will play two or three times that many. The benefits? *Maybe* kids become better ball players. But at what cost? One study compared the SAT scores of two groups of high school athletes. One group's extracurricular activities were only sports. The other group participated in a diversity of activities. The SAT scores were *lower* for kids involved in sports only. A child who narrowly focuses on sports may be weakened in other ways.

Our children have important skills to acquire—they must learn how to care for others, to connect with God, to manage money, and to think critically. To help our kids meet these needs, we made sure that they were involved in a broad mix of activities: household chores, church camp, mission trips, family gatherings, gardening (at home and with Grandpa), growing and selling produce, helping neighbors, and more.

Psychologist John Rosemond has reported that, when he speaks to parent groups, he asks them to raise a hand if they did chores as a child. Almost all of them raise a hand. But when he asks them to raise a hand if they require their kids to do regular chores, only a few raise their hands. Chores help train a child for the future. As an adult he will need to know how to wash clothes, clean a bathroom, fix a meal, care for a lawn, budget money, etc. When our boys complained about household chores ("Why do we have to weed the garden? Our friends aren't their parents' slaves!"), we would try to calmly explain: "Family life is a joint effort. If you don't help out, then some other member of this family will be unfairly burdened." Parents, if you *don't* treat your child like a privileged houseguest, your future son- or daughter-in-law will shower you with praise!

Quiet Times

Mary, the mother of Jesus, was an ordinary young woman with an extraordinary faith. What was the source of that faith? The Bible tells us that she *pondered* what was happening to her and *treasured all these things in her heart.* But what child today has time to ponder anything?! We keep kids busy, busy, busy. Think about it; how often do you tell your child to hurry up? We parents are rightly worried about the dangers of drugs and alcohol for our children. But a greater, more subtle danger may be a busy life. A child needs time to play by himself, to daydream, to draw a picture, to read a book, and to pray. The only way to give this to your child is to limit his activities. Otherwise he may come to look and act like a tired businessman.

Some parents enroll their child in sports early, fearing that she will fall behind her peers if she starts later. But putting off a child's entry into *organized* sports doesn't mean that she can't begin playing. As a parent, you can teach some beginning skills better than a team can. For example, if you help her to practice her batting, she can hit a ball fifty times (if you have the energy to chase those balls!). But, in a team practice, she might be limited to five to ten swings. Furthermore, as educator Emily Greenspan observes, "an organized game is seldom the best place to learn skills because a child must learn to perform skills under pressure before he is comfortable with the sport. The child who just wants to learn how to pick up a ground ball and throw it correctly to first base is confounded by the fact that he has to throw out the runner and kill a rally."

Can families limit a child to one sport per athletic season? Some worry that a child's talent may go untapped ("My son is already playing soccer, but I better sign him up for golf lessons, too. Who knows, he may be the next Tiger Woods!"). But would it have been a tragedy if Tiger Woods's parents had missed his golf talent? John Rosemond commented on that possibility: "Maybe Tiger would have grown up to become a virologist, and maybe he would have discovered a cure for [a major disease]." We need parents who have a larger vision than the next championship trophy.

WHAT: CHOOSING A SPORT

Rugby underwent major rule changes in the nineteenth century. Thomas Tutko listed a few of those changes:

- Rule XIV. No hacking with the heel, unless below the knee.

- Rule XV. No one wearing projecting nails or iron plates on the soles of his shoes or boots shall be allowed to play.

- Rule XXII. A player standing up to another may hold one arm only, but he may hack him or knock the ball out of his hands if he attempts to kick it.

Imagine being a parent with such choices—it might have been safer to send your son to war! Fortunately, we have a host of enjoyable and safe sports for children. But how do we choose?

Think about a Child's Need for Success

Before you decide whether to sign your child up for baseball or basketball, it is important to remember what is primary: *young children need to succeed.* Sports psychologist William Beausay explains:

> *All children need a series of happy, victorious experiences. The normal defeats will come in the routine give-and-take of their own play. But they must learn to succeed before they can accept defeat. After thirteen, they then must be defeated to instigate further growth.*

Success is important for a young child because he can't reason that if he fails, he will be good at some other sport or other activity.

A child's success will be greater in a sport that fits his talents. As a child athlete, our Andrew had the endurance of a South Dakota winter; even his brothers were impressed with his stamina on bike rides. Soccer was a perfect fit for him.

I recently saw an e-mail address that included the words "raising swimmers." Is someone forcing an identity on the whole family? Would a child in that family be allowed to pursue golf or soccer? One psychologist has written that girls who are allowed to pursue "their true interests are two steps ahead of the game. Teens who believe their parents have hopes for them that are *in line with their actual talents and passions*—feel most equipped" for the future.

Think about Exercise

Medical experts report an alarming increase in heart problems for the young—a problem lessened by vigorous exercise. If your child is interested in a sport like bowling, you might encourage her to swim or bike as well. Since the benefits of exercise are temporary, my wife and I wanted to establish the *habit* of exercise in our kids. Thus, our routines included physical activity. Our vacations included hiking and swimming; we biked to restaurants; we kicked a soccer ball or threw a Frisbee while dinner was being prepared; we walked our cocker spaniel (whose idea of fetching a stick was to run away from us and see if we could catch him!).

Parents, turn in your chauffeur license and let your child bike or walk herself to school, to ball practice, or to a friend's house. (The media's fixation on the rare child abduction has led many parents to be overly protective of their children. The Polly Klaas Foundation reports that in the entire U.S. there are about 100 kids abducted by a stranger each year and half of those eventually return home.)

Think about a Lifetime

My sons stumbled a bit as they made the transition from childhood fitness (when they were in top shape) to adult fitness (when they struggled). This happened partly because their childhood conditioning was rooted in team sports. Bruce Svare believes we have placed too much emphasis on team sports: "American sports culture is based on highly-organized team sports that make a very positive contribution to our social culture, but do little for our personal health and well-being." Think about the sports that you see people playing in their fifties, sixties, and beyond: tennis, golf, racquetball, swimming, running, and bicycling. There aren't many football leagues for senior citizens! Since exercise should be a part of the entire span of life, encourage your child to learn at least one of these lifetime sports.

Think about Physical Health

Each year, over four million kids visit emergency rooms as a result of sports injuries—a fourfold increase since 1995! As kids' sports have hit "the fast lane" with longer seasons, more sports, and harder training, young bodies have suffered.

Children's hearts cause only minor concern, since they can withstand nearly any test of endurance. But the *overuse* of joints (e.g., shoulders and knees) can cause serious damage, because the bones of preteen kids are still growing. The problem with overuse injuries is that some are hard to detect: no blood, no bruises, no broken bones. Even X-rays or MRIs may not reveal anything. As a result, parents have to depend on their child's self-report. "But what if my child is faking it?" Even if he is, he may be telling you something important; for some reason, he doesn't want to compete.

In former days, children often played sports without adults present. If a child hurt his arm throwing a baseball, he probably went home and rested it. But now he has multiple coaches and his parents to please. He hears them say foolish things like, "You just need to learn how to play through the pain." Our eldest son played basketball and soccer on ankles that hadn't healed properly and he can no longer play those sports.

Some sports, like football, are more likely to cause injuries. A boy who played high-school football in 2006 in South Dakota was seven times more likely to receive a season-ending injury than a boy playing basketball! Two years later, the University of Georgia lost nineteen football players to season-ending injuries.

A chief concern in football is the potential for concussions. One survey found that 61% of NFL players had experienced at least one concussion, and one-fourth of them had had three or more. Those who had concussions reported increased problems with memory, concentration, speech impediments, and headaches. Another study reported that the prevalence of Alzheimer's among retired NFL players was far more than the national average— nineteen times the rate for men from ages thirty through forty-nine!

Fortunately, football officials are listening to these statistics. The NFL instituted stricter rules on managing concussions, requiring players who show signs of a concussion to be removed from (at least) the rest of the game. High schools have also taken a tougher stand. Referees nationwide must remove players who show *any* sign of a concussion, and not just when an athlete loses consciousness. If trainers even suspect a concussion, the player may not return to the game. Unfortunately, many high schools don't have a doctor or athletic trainer present to evaluate athletes. Some schools claim that they can't afford a trainer. But one expert believes "that means you can't afford to have a program. The presence of a certified athletic trainer makes your program safer by every measure, and if you can't afford to make the program safe, then you should be closing it up."

Am I on a crusade to ban football? Not at all. Injury is a risk in any sport. (And even outside of sports—my nephew, while playing college football, tore his ACL walking down the stairs!) Though we encouraged our boys to play safer sports, if they had been passionate about playing football, we may have said "Yes."

Injuries can be lessened if parents understand how a particular sport stresses children's bodies. For example:

- Preteen runners should run no more than three miles a day, because the growth plates at the ends of bones are vulnerable to injury.

- Soccer and basketball players may need extra support for their ankles with all of their stopping, starting, and cutting.

- Baseball pitchers, especially in the preteen years, should have their innings strictly limited.

- Some medical experts believe that young female runners who overtrain are more vulnerable to injury than boys, because their bodies mature differently.

- Don't let your *young* child specialize. She should play a variety of sports, because each sport will stress different body parts.

Finally, Dr. Stuart Brown, who directs the National Institute for Play, believes that risk is an important part of children's play: "I don't want to foster broken bones and concussions. But an inherent part of being playful is taking risk. What you don't want to do is have the risks be excessive." He is concerned about parents who hover over their kids, thus limiting their freedom to explore, to risk. He observes that children's playgrounds demonstrate this overconcern: "There are no teeter totters and most of the swings don't really go very high, and the monkey bars can only be three feet high. You know, it's reasonable to have safe playgrounds, but it's also reasonable to have challenging playgrounds." When we are overly protective of our kids, we may be "keeping their bodies safe while we are endangering their souls."

Think about Mental Health

A child's mental health can be significantly impacted by sports.

Here are some issues to consider when choosing a sport:

The League. Educator Bruce Svare wisely points out that a "youth sports program should be judged on the basis of how it treats its *least talented kids,* not on how it treats its most talented kids." I would avoid a sports program that doesn't legislate ample playing time for young kids.

The Coaches. One study found that youth hockey and baseball coaches rated having fun considerably higher than swimming, wrestling, and gymnastics coaches. Furthermore, baseball, basketball, soccer, and hockey coaches rated winning significantly lower than did wrestling coaches. These results only suggest trends. It is best to check out a coach to see what emphasis he puts on winning, having fun, and developing skills.

Advanced vs. Recreational. Children's sports today are often organized into advanced and recreational leagues. The theory is that grouping athletes with similar skills together will produce a more uplifting experience. But one study of nine-year-olds found that kids who participated in recreational leagues viewed themselves more positively than did kids in advanced leagues. Though the research didn't explore why this was true, could it be that the recreational leagues emphasize winning less? Some kids don't want to play sports seriously, preferring fewer practices and modest competition. Don't push them to a greater commitment.

Stress. Moderate levels of stress usually enhance a child's experience; kids enjoy the excitement. But high levels can be damaging to their emotional health. As expected, individual sports create more stress than do team sports. If you lose a golf match, you can't blame your teammates. If your golf ball goes out of bounds, guess who hit it there?! A study of girls competing in eight different sports found that gymnastics was the most stressful, followed by track and field, swimming, tennis, softball, volleyball, basketball, and field hockey. Do winning athletes handle the stress better? No. Studies have found no correlation between anxiety and a child's ability. Better athletes may be burdened by higher expectations.

Cathy and I were pleased with our sons' involvement in soccer, partly because of its lower stress. Standing on a soccer field, a young child can watch the clouds fly by or search for a four-leaf clover, but few people (other than the child's parents!) will notice. On the other hand, former Olympic ice-skating champion, Peggy Fleming, explained the stress in her sport: "In four minutes of free skating you're being judged on a whole year of practice. Not many sports put you through that, being the focal point of the entire arena. You've got to look like you're enjoying yourself and accept the judges' decision and not throw a tomato at them. It's tough." Because of the stress of individual sports, it might be best to guide your *young* child toward team sports. She can begin learning the individual sports with minimal direct competition.

WHAT: SHOULD MY CHILD
JOIN A SELECT TEAM?

Our three boys played on select soccer teams. I coached our youngest son's team for six years. Though it was a mostly positive experience for us, I'm not sure that it would be in today's select system. My primary concern is that these teams have amped up the time and commitment required. As a result, many youth sports have become serious business. If your child wants to play for one of these teams, consider these issues:

Watch over Your Child's Whole Development
Just because a child has talent does *not* mean that you are obliged to enroll her in a select program. As I stated earlier, look at all of your child's needs and see how that particular commitment fits into her whole development.

Watch out for Specialization
If your child plays one sport nearly all year, it will greatly increase his odds of developing an overuse injury. Even professional baseball pitchers rest their arms during the winter.

Furthermore, narrowly focusing on one sport may not even produce the best athletes. A Division I college soccer coach notes that "Hands down, the best kids in our program ... have been kids who have played three sports, who have had balance, who maybe started late in soccer but they're really enjoying it and they can develop."

Watch What Develops

Though it may be painful to extricate your child from her commitment to a team, have the courage to live out your convictions. Is the coach too harsh? The schedule too demanding? Are your child's academics faltering? Your child may initially object to being withdrawn, but later, when she has her life back, she will probably thank you.

Watch Your Motives

Don't let your child become a surrogate for your dreams. This is his life, not yours!

Watch Your Expectations

Parents may view the time and money that they spend on their child's sport as an investment—and investors want returns! After one top athlete in our city underperformed when compared to Dad's expectations, her father told her: "If we're going to spend all this money and travel to tournaments, you better work more on your game."

The return that many parents of select athletes are hoping for is a college scholarship. Though NCAA schools award about one billion dollars for athletic scholarships, they offer over thirty billion dollars for academic scholarships! These statistics led one sports leader to wisely advise, "If you want to get money from a scholarship, go home and read to your children every night!"

WHAT: ELITE ATHLETES

The elite of the elite are those who train with professional coaches, hoping to become an Olympic athlete or the next Serena Williams. One teenage swimmer who was training for the Olympics had a weekday schedule in which she swam from 5:30—7:00 AM, rushed to school, returned home at 1:30, caught a nap, ate dinner at 3:00, worked out again from 4:30—7:30, crawled home, ate a snack, completed her homework, and fell into bed. On weekends she labored even longer hours.

Some of these elite athletes with Olympic potential move a thousand miles away from home to live with a master coach, only seeing their families on an occasional weekend. Though they may become superior athletes, will it help them grow into happy, fulfilled adults? Maybe not.

Conclusion

Our boys did not start playing organized sports until they were seven years old. If we were raising our kids today, I still believe that seven is a good age at which to begin *organized* sports. Limiting their involvement is not only good for family life, but it is also better for children's long-term involvement with sports. Children who begin early tend to drop out early. They may be rebelling against a childhood consumed by sports.

CHAPTER FIVE

Organizing Children's Sports

"We've got all the wrong priorities. Why do we have traveling teams with fancy uniforms cutting kids at young ages?"

—Wayne Harris, sports psychologist

The structure of children's games is a critical factor in determining what kind of experience children have in sports. Hall-of-Fame pitcher, Robin Roberts, concluded that ball games for preteens should be "a softball thrown overhand where a boy can hit fifteen times a game, with no walks and strikeouts. They should be running and sliding into bases. The score should be 42-38."

De-emphasize Winning

Your daughter is ready to shoot the first of two free throws. Time has expired and her team is trailing by a single point. Her free throws may determine whether her team wins or loses. What if she misses them both? Will she be crushed by her failure? The answer, in part, depends on the importance of the game. Sports research has concluded that competing is fun when winning isn't a life-or-death matter. A girl can handle the disappointment of missing crucial free throws if the game is not being played for the championship of the galaxy!

Researchers observed professional football games to record acts of assistance between opponents (e.g., helping a player off of the ground). During regular season games, help was frequently given. But during the Super Bowl that year, there was not a single incident of helping. The structure of the game had not changed, only its meaning. When my boys anticipated playing in a championship game, I tried to avoid frequent conversations about it because the more the outcome is stressed, the more stress it puts on the athletes.

Thus, sports should be organized *in the early years* to de-emphasize winning. Many youth programs (up until the age of seven or eight) don't keep score and, thus, don't have standings or tournaments or championships. Some of these leagues choose to eliminate trophies, medals, MVP awards, all-star teams, and award banquets because these also accentuate the winners and losers.

Even at the select-team level winning should be a goal, not *the* goal. When I was organizing my twelve-year-old son's select soccer team, I was advised by other coaches to limit my commitment to these preteen boys to one year at a time. They warned that puberty would change their bodies in unpredictable ways. I chose *not* to follow this advice. I told the boys that if they were faithful to their commitments—attending practices and games, helping to raise money, maintaining a coachable attitude, controlling their on-field behavior—I would maintain my commitment to them. I wanted those boys to be assured that I would *never* drop them just to make room for another player. I also went against those coaches' advice in scheduling tournaments (we played in five to six, not eight to ten, each year) and off-season practices (we eliminated them). I believe that God honored those child-friendly commitments by giving us success on the field; we won a boxful of trophies over the next seven years.

Adopt Must-Play Rules

Must-play rules should be adopted and enforced for preteen athletes. Ninety percent of a group of children indicated that they would rather play on a losing team than sit on the bench of a winning team. Kids want to play. Let them play.

It is ironic that, even if early sports programs were designed to develop Olympic champions, a policy of playing the best is not wise. A twelve-year study revealed that only one in four children who were stars in childhood were also stars in adolescence. The boys who dominated my sons' sports in the preteen years did so mostly because their bodies matured early. When the other boys caught up, they often surpassed the early bloomers in talent and performance.

Even on my son's select team, I let every boy play for a significant number of minutes. Did it hurt us? No. I think it helped us. Since all of the boys felt like contributors, we had high team morale. Furthermore, in weekend tournaments, our players were often more rested for championship games than were teams who only played their best. Our boys' fresher bodies enabled them to frequently beat more talented teams.

Must-play rules alone won't ensure a good experience for kids. Some coaches have evaded rules of equal play by asking certain kids to stay home from an important game. Or they have given grudging acceptance of the rule: "Oh, no, Smith hasn't played yet? I guess he has to go in." Such insults may be designed to get young Smith to quit the team.

Are there any limits to this "all-play" policy? Yes, especially during the teen years. At a recent high-school basketball game, I was sitting next to the parents of a senior boy on the team. Their son was not very skilled and had not worked to increase his skills. Near the end of a lopsided game, his parents groused that their son had barely played. But should he ever play significantly? In the same way that we wouldn't expect the school orchestra to select a novice flute player for a solo, we shouldn't expect uncommitted and untalented athletes to receive much playing time on school teams. (There are other leagues for them.) If this senior plays, it cuts playing time for the dedicated underclassmen who will form the backbone of future teams.

Minimize Organization

When my older sons began to play football against each other, the games ended quickly because the elder was consistently beating the younger, who opted to not play rather than lose. When the older one complained about his brother's refusal to play, I explained that he would have to adjust the rules to entice his brother to play. A few days later, the two of them came bursting through the back door with a football. The elder proclaimed that his younger brother had beaten him. Amazed, I asked how it had happened. The younger one, beaming, explained: "Well, he had to tackle me. I only had to touch him." That night I was able to tell my eldest how proud I was—and Jesus was—of his efforts to make the game fun for his brother.

My boyhood was filled with minimally organized sports. We played pick-up basketball, baseball, and football. When we didn't have enough players for full baseball teams, we played a game that we invented called "California." All hits had to clear the infield in the air or you were out. Thus, infielders were mostly unnecessary.

Where have these childhood games gone? Most kids today don't play sports unless it is organized by adults. Though it is unrealistic to think that organized sports will suddenly disappear, the best solution may be to offer less organized alternatives. On one sizzling summer day when our boys were young, I had spent the morning doing yard work and by late morning, was hot, sweaty, and ready for a break. My sons easily talked me into a trip to the swimming pool. But they did not share my vision of snoozing by the pool, interrupted only by an occasional cooling dunk. They coaxed me into playing a game of "keep away" with their friends. Though the age span was around forty years, it didn't keep any of us from having a grand time. We raced after stray throws. We leaped out of the water to try to block an opponent's toss. We delighted in seeing the smaller ones miraculously steal the ball from the bigger ones. My youngest, Jered, who didn't even know how to swim then, was joyously bobbing in the midst of all that activity with an inner tube around his middle. That swimming pool was filled with more joy than water. How could we have had more fun? By establishing a league and finding coaches and conducting practices and writing a rule book and keeping standings and—how ridiculous! But it isn't far from what we have done to many children's games. Kids don't need uniforms and referees to have an enjoyable experience.

Teach Skills

Bruce Svare, a professor of psychology and a longtime participant in youth sports, formerly believed that scheduling many games was the way to maximize athletic talent. He now believes that youth coaches should focus more on teaching skills. As a result, the basketball program that he leads has a new mission statement: "We are a league principally interested in participation and improving basketball skills." Svare's league cut back on the number of tournaments and games and increased the number of practices and clinics. Svare wonders if Americans' diminished emphasis on fundamentals may be the reason why the rest of the basketball world has caught up with us in basketball.

When I began as the coach of my son's select soccer team,

I knew relatively little about soccer (*slightly* more than I knew about heart surgery!). One of the wisest decisions that our team made was to send the boys and me to a soccer clinic for one week each summer. Those annual clinics enabled me to learn the basics of the sport with the boys.

The development of kids' skills will be enhanced by letting them play multiple positions. One football coach explained: "Running the ball, throwing it, catching a pass, making touchdowns—those are the things kids think of as football." Letting kids play multiple positions also agrees with their long-term development. Many who are too slow or too small to play a certain position may not be so when their bodies mature. But be careful; while coaching a soccer team for young boys, I let an untested boy play goalie and the other team scored three quick goals. He was so distraught that he almost quit the team.

Equalize Teams

I have played basketball at our local "Y" for the past five decades. For many years, there was a group of skilled players who all arrived at the same time so that they could play on the same team. The results were frequently lopsided. Though it may have been fun for them (I don't really understand why crushing your opponent in a pick-up game is fun!), it certainly was not fun for the rest of us.

Research has confirmed that competing is fun when kids feel that they have a chance to win. Watch what happens when a team is a recurrent loser. The kids may not put out much effort. They may bicker among themselves. Practices may be poorly attended.

Some sports leagues have developed a draft to counter inequality (And these drafts should take place annually, so that no team can stockpile the best players.). One coach explained the impact that a draft had on his league: "Something happened. We got along great the whole year. The league was tight, and I think we all had fun. I know my kids did. You'd see 'em during a game running back to the huddle, and sliding in on their pads. It didn't look like the Dolphins, but it was fun."

Some leagues split players between "recreational" and "advanced" divisions. When the better players are grouped in their own league, the less-skilled kids improve their skills with more opportunities to pitch or kick or play quarterback. Teams can also be organized according to size and weight, especially in contact sports. It isn't safe for a 60-pound boy to try to tackle a 120-pound boy!

Develop Creative Structures

Some believe that tampering with the rules of a game is like editing the Ten Commandments. But rules should be adjusted to meet young children's needs. When our boys were preteens, we had a basket in the driveway that was about eight-and-a-half feet tall (I take supreme offense at any suggestion that I set the basket height so that I could feel like the 6'10" player that I always wanted to be!). It may not be a coincidence that all three of my boys became accurate shooters. Many basketball hoops now come with the ability to lower the basket so that kids don't have to strain to shoot the ball to the rim.

Here are some other suggestions about what has been done or could be done to improve sports for young children:

- Don't allow a full court press in basketball, because young kids can't throw the long passes that break a press.

- Youth basketball games are often cut to five- or six-minute quarters. Why? Since only five players can play at one time, many kids go home having played only ten to twelve minutes. Put the quarters back at eight minutes (or longer!) to give kids more playing time.

- Play soccer games with a small number of players on a small field. The kids are much more involved than they would be with a larger team on a larger field.

- Use a pitching machine, or an adult to pitch, in youth baseball games.

- Don't allow walks or strikeouts in baseball, so that kids get more practice in hitting and fielding.

- Limit the number of pitches that a pitcher throws. In one study, nearly 50% of eleven and twelve-year-old pitchers complained of arm pain.

Conclusion

While I was coaching my son's select soccer team, a coach from another top team in our age division proposed that we combine teams to create a powerhouse in our region. Though tempted,

I quickly rejected it. All of my boys had dedicated themselves
to our team. How could I dump some of them so that others
could compete at a higher level? Bruce Svare has observed that
competitive sports are increasingly organized to "satisfy the
needs of a small group of elite athletes, while recreational and
fitness-based sports, which satisfy the needs of the vast majority, have been deemphasized." Part of this coach's justification
for combining the teams was to give the boys more exposure
to college coaches and, thus, the opportunity to win college
scholarships. But only 4-5% of the nation's seven million high
school athletes will earn scholarships for sports. Children's athletics should be organized primarily for that 95% majority.

CHAPTER SIX
Coaches and Coaching

"One of the great myths in America is that sports build character. They can and they should.... But sports don't build character unless a coach possesses character and intentionally teaches it."

— Joe Ehrmann, Coach & Former NFL Lineman

"It's not about winning and losing. It's about developing relationships and getting close to [your players]."

— Mike Krzyzewski, Duke Basketball Coach

During my sophomore year of high school I tried out for the school's basketball team—along with 120 other boys! At the first practice, we were divided into two groups based on our junior high coaches' judgments. I was placed in the "let's-cut-them-quickly" group. By the end of the first week, I was one of two boys left from that group! And, by the end of the season, I was playing with the best fifteen players. I have Coach Ben

Newcomb to thank for my survival and promotion. He alone saw and encouraged the talent that I had. Though he yelled and threw clipboards and kicked chairs—mostly in response to my errors!—I loved him and his discipline because he believed in me. His coaching nurtured a passion for basketball and, more importantly, a confidence that if I worked hard I could accomplish an important goal.

But I also had negative experiences with coaches. When I was in the fourth grade, I tried out for a Little League team. On the day when cuts were announced, I was one of the boys cut. As I dejectedly climbed on my bike, the coach asked if I would lead calisthenics. I agreed, wondering if I was being given a second chance. When we were done, I stood around not knowing what to do next. But the coach said, "That's all, Schock; you can leave now." I felt humiliated in front of the other boys. Had the coach intended that? I don't know.

During the twenty to twenty-five years when my boys were competing in youth sports, I was a coach and an observer of coaches. Both sides of the coaching experience offer unique opportunities to live out our faith and influence kids' development.

KIDS AND THEIR COACHES

Over the past three to four decades I have had hundreds of conversations with parents about their kids' sporting experiences; probably the majority of them have been about their kids' coaches. Some have been frustrated, others furious, many confounded by actions that these coaches took or did not take. It's important to remember that the goal for our children is maturity, not playing time. We want them to grow in their walk with God through *all* of their experiences in sports.

Be Realistic

One of our sons played on his school's varsity basketball team with a boy who had little talent. The coach didn't cut him because he knew that the boy desperately wanted to make the team. Even though the boy was content to ride the bench, his parents frequently grumbled about their son's lack of playing time.

When parents don't accurately assess their child's abilities, they, and often their child, become frustrated. Since it is hard for a parent to be objective, I occasionally asked sports-wise people to appraise my sons' talents. I used that information to help my sons (and me!) develop reasonable expectations. One time we used the information to begin praying that our son would have an opportunity to play more—a prayer that God eventually answered.

Be a Grown-Up

When Nathan was a senior in high school and a starter on his basketball team, his playing time was reduced for a few games because his coach believed that he wasn't hustling. This made no sense. His athletic intensity never dropped much below ten, as evidenced by six steals in his last game! So what was the best way to help my son? If the goal was his maturity, I couldn't lead him where I hadn't traveled. Though I wanted to gripe about his "brain-dead coach" (the description that kept assaulting my mind!), I chose to forgive the coach and help my son to do the same.

Be a Friend

Coaching can be a lonely calling. What your child's coach may need is a friend—someone who will encourage him, drive a van, assist at a practice, record statistics, etc. The main communication most coaches hear is how they could do their jobs better (How do you think your surgeon would react if you gave him advice about your upcoming surgery?!).

Be Patient

The world is filled with injustice, as the Apostle Peter reminds us: *Dear friends, don't be surprised at the painful trial you are suffering, as though something strange were happening to you.* Sports provide rich opportunities for kids to learn how to endure and grow through trials. When my eldest was a junior on his high-school basketball team, he played behind a boy whom he had beaten twice in the pre-season, one-on-one tournaments 7-0! We were all discouraged until we remembered that sports can be the classroom in which to learn the *patient endurance* that grounds a spiritual life. One psychologist believes that older kids' self-confidence "grows primarily through overcoming adversity." The Apostle James echoed this theme: *Count it pure joy, my brothers, whenever you face trials of many kinds, because you know that the testing of your faith develops perseverance* (James 1:2). Help your child to see his adversity as a test of his young faith.

Be Wise

One of the dilemmas that parents face is whether to intervene between a child and her coach. The answer is "sometimes"—especially for preteens. When one of our sons was eleven years old, he played on a soccer team whose coaches were shorting him and other boys on mandated playing time. We asked if they realized what was happening. They said "no" and promised to do better. But when the situation didn't improve, we reported the coaches to the league. League officials' presence at the next few games corrected the abuse of the discouraged boys.

But as kids age, they need to learn how to handle their own conflicts. Child expert Diane Ehrensaft in her book, *Spoiling Childhood,* explains:

> *We have over problem-solved for our children. We rush in and sweep up the gravel on life's road and eliminate any opportunity for our children to work through difficulty and come out on the other side, knowing they have solved a problem and can do it again.*

Initially, your child might be reluctant to talk with her coach, but you can help her to think through what she wants to say and how to say it. When our son Jered was disappointed with his playing time on his basketball team, he met with his coach to ask how he could improve. This enabled him to focus on skills that eventually led to more playing time.

THE PARENT AS COACH

The job description for coaching youth sports should read as follows:

- Hours: Mostly evenings and weekends, with a minimum of ten to fifeen hours per week. Applicant must be willing to forgo vacations and other leisure activities.

- Main Responsibilities: To develop the character of, act as role model for, and improve sports skills in children.

- Qualifications: Someone with perfect patience.

- Experience required: None. (Those with experience seldom re-apply!)

- Pay: Nothing.

If that job description were published, who would apply? In truth, the commitment to coaching youngsters is a high-paying job whose dividends often endure in treasured memories. A sampling of mine include

- A beaming seven-year-old boy handing me a folded picture of a basketball player: "Here, coach, this is for you."

- Barely losing to the number-one team in our soccer league (even though we were three players short) because I was able to teach young boys how to run an offside trap. My son, Jered, who played goalkeeper, couldn't have been more thrilled than if we had won the World Cup.

- The father who wrote "When you first asked Joe to play on your team, he was about the happiest guy in the universe. He had an emotional need to be noticed in some type of sport. You recognized his abilities, as ragged as they were, and his spirits soared. No one had noticed him before, and that was frustrating for him. He so enjoyed playing for you and the team. You're in my Hall of Fame!"

- When my soccer defender scored the winning goal for our opponent, our players comforted, rather than condemned, him.

- Winning a championship game over a team with a reputation for running up the score on other teams.

One of coaching's greatest personal dividends was how it built my relationships with my boys. But coaching also allowed me to build relationships with my sons' teammates, who came mostly from non-Christian homes. At a time when most unbelievers hold a dim view of the church, the sports fields provide a place where Christians' lights can shine. When my team traveled, I offered a worship opportunity on Saturday evening or Sunday morning at our motel. Most of the boys and some of the parents participated. Those experiences of explaining God's truth to these un-churched boys may have contributed to my adult sons' mature relationships with non-Christians; they are *in the world but not of the world.*

THE GOALS FOR COACHES

Build Relationships

In my first season as a soccer coach, I had a beginner who was a head shorter than the other boys. During our first game, some of my players teased and punched this boy before I could stop them. He never returned. After that experience, I became dedicated to helping kids to build affirming relationships with their teammates. One way in which I did this was by accentuating the unique contribution of each child. For example, at a season-ending, parent-son potluck, I gave ribbons to all the boys on my sixth-grade basketball team. The awards stressed their individual strengths: "Most Steals," "Best Rebounder," "Most Improved Player," "Best Passer," etc. I let the boys guess who would receive each award. They were right, in most cases, and were genuinely enthusiastic about each other's awards.

When a coach doesn't recognize the individuality of his players, it often hurts the team. One of our sons played on a soccer team whose coaches believed they had two stars and not much else. Their season-long strategy of requiring the bit players to feed the ball to the lead players was disastrous. The supporting cast lost its confidence and its freedom, and the stars stumbled under such weighty expectations.

But it isn't just in-team relationships that are important. Some coaches motivate their teams by making the opponents sound like Gestapo agents! I tried to counter this competitive tension by getting to know the other coaches in our league.

Then I could phone a coach to compliment his team's progress, or share coaching tips if he was a novice.

After years of coaching, I had become weary and considered retiring. But I asked myself, "What would I replace it with? Would I spend more of my summers in self-absorbed leisure?" I concluded that I could do few things more important than giving myself to these kids.

Encourage Independence

Coaches encourage independence in their athletes by including them in the decision-making process. While I was coaching a middle-high basketball team, the league suspended the equal-play rule during a city tournament. I decided to let the boys decide: "Play only your starters, thus increasing your odds of winning, or play everyone?" They voted to play their best. As a result, the bench players were enthusiastic supporters of the starters during the tournament.

As kids age, they should participate in the decisions about when and how much to practice, what drills to use, the number of tournaments to enter, and what positions they will play. The goal for coaches is to help kids learn how to manage their own lives.

Teach Character

The University of Texas basketball team suffered a narrow defeat when a player failed to rebound a last-second shot and his opponent tipped it in for a two-point victory. After the game,

Texas's coach, Rick Barnes, noticed that this player was hanging his head, so he called him into his office:

"Boogie, why do you think we lost?"

"Because I got beat on the last play."

"Wrong. Because we all made mistakes. I made mistakes; the other guys made mistakes. We're all human. We all make mistakes. We're going to make some more of them this week. But you can't wallow in it. You pick yourself up and go on to the next play, the next day, the next game."

Knowing that this player had recently lost his father, Barnes added, "The death of your father was worth crying about. But losing a basketball game is not." Sports give coaches many opportunities to teach what is truly valuable.

Develop Skills

Coaching involves more than patting kids on the back. As kids advance in sports, their attitude toward competition is based more on actual performance. As a result, improving skills must be an essential goal of coaching—a task many of us need help to do. As a greenhorn soccer coach I attended numerous clinics in which I was taught technique, strategy, and drills by licensed coaches. If I were to grade my coaching today, I believe that I am a better soccer coach (a sport that I had never played) than a baseball or basketball coach (sports I was dedicated to). Knowing that I was ignorant when it came to soccer, I labored to overcome that ignorance. In the other sports, I often assumed that I knew more than I did!

When a basketball player makes a bad pass, what good does it do to shout, "Watch your passes!" Oh, really? Barking at her only erodes her confidence; she will now limit herself to safe passes. But a teacher will take the time to explain why she made a bad pass: "You picked up your dribble before you knew what you were going to do with the ball." A skilled coach instructs rather than whines.

As a coach teaches, he must be sure that his drills are age-appropriate. Consider the youth baseball coach who was observed hitting balls to his beginners.

> *Not one child fielded a grounder cleanly. So the ball would roll through their legs or bounce by them, and they'd run and chase it and bring the ball back. Then, inexplicably, the coach decided to hit fly balls to them, when not one of them had mastered grounders yet! He began hitting fly balls, and I'll never forget the looks on the faces of those children. They looked like they were in a war zone and planes were dropping bombs on them from above. They were doing everything that they could to dodge the balls.*

If we don't understand kids' age-appropriate capabilities, our instruction won't be very effective.

Pursue Success

Winning should not be the only measure of success. My players hungrily devoured the statistics that I kept (rebounds, assists, steals, baskets) during basketball games. This was the case with

Jacob, a large, lumbering boy who was assigned to my fifth-grade basketball team. At the first practice, his mother apologized twice for her boy's ineptitude. As the season developed, I noticed that her attitude had seeped into her son, who meekly deflected my compliments: "Oh, it wasn't such a good shot, just lucky." But Jacob was a hustler, and his size made him an adequate rebounder. As he saw his rebounding statistics improve, the personal put-downs faded, and Jacob became a happy, enthusiastic participant.

Though winning isn't *everything*, is also isn't *nothing*. After my select soccer team had competed for three or four years, it had become the second-best team in our state in its age division. The top team—whom we had never beaten—had successfully recruited several of our top players, some of whom then played little on their new team. Was that team trying to weaken our team? It appeared so. Thus, when we finally beat them in a championship game, it was particularly satisfying for the boys—and the coach! My wife incisively commented, "You beat a philosophy, not just a team."

Help Parents

One of the best ways to help parents is to communicate with them. I regularly scheduled meetings to talk with parents about philosophy, strategy, and plans. I let them talk to me about their concerns. Some parents pushed me to practice more, enter more tournaments, or practice in the off-season. I had to keep my focus on what was best for the boys and me. This wasn't my job!

Watch out for the parent who prowls the sidelines, growling commands like a marine sergeant. I often had to remind parents that I was the coach. They could shout encouragement, but not instructions.

Have Fun

What do you suppose our family dog added to (or should I say, subtracted from) a soccer scrimmage? As might be expected, he created the unexpected. His speed got him to the ball first, but it was impossible to predict in which direction he would headbutt it. When he tired of tackling the ball, he started tackling the kids. I wanted to send him home, but the boys begged to let him stay.

In a culture which takes winning too seriously, it is important for a coach to ask whether his kids are enjoying themselves. Fun can be nurtured by choosing drills carefully, by letting them play new positions, by visiting the Dairy Queen after practice, etc. Championships can only be won by a few. Fun can be "won" by all.

The Transformation of Coaches: Learning to Trust God

Nathan's basketball team had experienced a rough season, but it was improving. This progress continued in the season-ending city tournament as they upset one of the better teams in the first round. In their semifinal game, they lost a close game that they could have easily won. I was very disappointed, but my son and his teammates were only mildly upset. They knew that they had played well against a better team and they didn't need to win to feel good about themselves. I was learning to trust God to give the kids the experiences that they truly needed.

I also learned to trust God in other ways. When my son's select soccer team lost players, I had to find talented replacements. Once, one of my players invited a boy to our next tournament who was reportedly the skilled goalkeeper that we needed. I told him not to invite him until I had seen him play. But my player misunderstood me and invited the boy. He was a superb goalie and became our fulltime goalkeeper. Another time, a mom called who had recently moved to town. She was looking for a team for her son, who had played at a high level in Oklahoma. I mistakenly told her that he was too old. But she had the boldness to call me back and correct me. Her son became a key contributor to our team. God was meeting our needs in spite of my follies!

Coaching isn't just about the development of kids; it is also about the development of coaches! Coaching was often the means that God used to teach me important spiritual truths.

CHAPTER SEVEN

The Influence of the Sportsworld

"It struck me when I was on my way to play on my softball team and found myself fretting that I would miss listening to a crucial [Oakland] A's game. There I was, about to play in a real game with my friends—and I cared more about another game to be played by people I had never met. If I muffed a grounder and lost our game I would feel bad, but I would undoubtedly feel worse if the A's Alfredo Griffin ... booted his grounder and lost his game."

—Tim Stafford,
Senior Writer for *Christianity Today*

The devotion of Nebraskans to their football team is legendary. One fan labored to make his family's wardrobe reflect the team's color: "We have red in all weights of coats, all lengths of dresses, shirts, sport coats, slacks, jackets, shoes, boots, lined boots, hats, caps, scarves, sweaters, shorts, ties, gloves, mittens, socks, watches, pins, bracelets, earrings, and buttons." Such behavior led a cartoon salesman to quip: "If it won't sell, paint it red and send it to Nebraska."

A Husker fan's devotion isn't confined to a mere three to four months in the fall: "We expect news coverage from August practice, through the fall season, including bowl practice in December and the bowl game in January. We look at the lineups in March, follow spring practice in April and attend the spring Red-White squad game in May. Somehow we manage through June, but pro football, with some former Big Red players, starts in July, which carries us back to August practice."

The "sportsworld" is the combined influence of sports in our culture—the passion of fans, peer conversations, direct participation, video games, books, athletic clothing, and much, much more. Understanding the sportsworld is crucial, because the sportsworld imparts values. Ardent Nebraska fans, communities that trumpet athletic success, the adulation of professional athletes... All of these elements proclaim values. When a father devotes his weekends to televised sports, he doesn't consciously think "*Since these games are more important to me than my son, I'll watch the games and ignore my son.*" In fact, if asked which is more important, he might become indignant ("What a stupid question!"). But don't his choices indicate his true values?

The influence of the sportsworld is inescapable. When a child participates in a team sport, he and his parents choose that experience. But the influence of the broader sportsworld is not so easily controlled. Can a child evade his dad's zeal for NFL football? The sportsworld has a weighty influence on the development of children. It projects a magnetic model of the person that they should become (their character) and the profession that they should pursue (their vocation). It's more than just a game.

THE IDEAL ATHLETE:
THE SPORTSWORLD AND CHARACTER

Character is very important to God: *Make every effort to add to your faith, goodness; and to goodness, knowledge; and to knowledge, self-control; and to self-control, perseverance; and to perseverance, godliness; and to godliness, brotherly kindness; and to kindness, love* (2 Pet. 1:5-7). Plaques and trophies gather dust on a shelf. Character is something that we take with us and use every day of our lives. The sportsworld claims to build character in our children. But does it? And what type of character does it seek to develop?

Persistence

Persistence is a primary theme in many athletes' stories. Shortly after beginning his major-league career, Mickey Mantle was demoted to the minor leagues. When he informed his dad that he was thinking about quitting, he hoped that his dad would say, "Oh, don't be silly, you're just in a little slump, you'll be all right, you're great." Instead, "he just looked at me for a second and then in a quiet voice that cut me in two he said, 'Well, Mick, if that's all the guts you have I think you better quit.'" (*The Quality of Courage*)

The number of slogans used to peddle persistence indicates the perceived importance of this trait:

- When the going gets tough, the tough get going.

- A winner never quits; a quitter never wins.

- If at first you don't succeed, try, try again.

Though persistence is often a healthy trait, there are difficulties between with how it is defined and how it is applied in the sportsworld.

Persistence and Life's Purpose

Hall-of-Fame coach Don Shula praised his star quarterback Dan Marino as a man who had "simple tastes and a simple goal." He wanted to be "the best quarterback in the NFL." But can life be narrowed to a "simple," single goal? What about Dan's marriage? His health? His relationship with God?

We call a businessman with a constricted vision a "workaholic." We call an athlete with a similar narrow focus dedicated. The successful life doesn't sacrifice everything for only one thing. The Spirit-led life is a process of juggling our roles as children, parents, mentors, husbands, wives, brothers, friends, workers, etc. God wants us to persevere in all of these tasks.

Persistence and Success

A defensive tackle explained how his team won a goal-line battle: "It was just a matter of who wanted it more." But was it strictly a matter of determination? Did their preparation make any difference? Did they merely guess where the other team would run the ball? Is it possible that they had more skilled players? Sportsworld messages often give the impression that persistence is all that is required for success.

One summer, during college, I worked as a door-to-door salesman. Our sales instructors drilled into us that there are two kinds of men—those who find a way and those who make an excuse. We were told that some would succeed because they were determined to overcome any obstacles. Others would fail, blaming the weather, the territory, or other factors. Though our trainers preached that hard work would ensure success, hard work was only one of many factors that determined success. I was a "success" because I had a car, I could socialize quickly with new people, and I had a good mentor. For many of the twnty-five percent who did not complete the summer, it was a shattering experience because they believed that they lacked the character to endure. Success requires more than persistence.

Persistence and Quitting

"Winners never quit." Don't they? Of course they do. Ronald Reagan quit acting to become a politician. The Wright brothers quit school to focus on their inventions. Peter quit fishing (twice!) to follow Jesus. Quitting may be a wise choice for the person who recognizes that God has better ways for him to invest his time. Today, many of our overscheduled, exhausted kids need to quit something. Help them do it.

Selflessness

The ideal athlete wishes his teammates well. Such selflessness is a good trait, but not if it sacrifices honesty. Former major-league pitcher Jim Bouton, in his book, *Ball Four,* was uncommonly honest about his feelings toward his pitching teammate during a spring training game:

> *His curve wasn't sharp and he was walking a lot of guys. He's got about eight kids and spring training means more to him than a lot of other guys. I felt sorry for him, but not very. Let me explain. It was rather early to be playing an intrasquad game and I thought, "I hope nobody gets hurt." Then I had to amend that. I meant "I hope I don't get hurt." I've always wanted everyone to do well. But I don't want them to do well at my expense.... It's not exactly the perfect attitude, but it's the way I feel.*

No, it is not a perfect attitude—but a common one among athletes. When we grant kids the freedom to voice their genuine feelings, then we can guide them toward true selflessness.

Self-Control

The self-controlled athlete doesn't crack under pressure. He is the golfer who rebounds with a birdie after a double-bogey, or the quarterback who engineers a last-minute winning score.

> *Unfortunately, self-control has often been meagerly defined as a lack of emotion. I often hear parents tell a banged-up child: "Oh, don't cry. You'll be alright." But what is so shameful*

about tears? Suppose on a visit to my home you slip on a patch of ice and fall flat on your back. And while you are trying to recover, I stand over you and bark, "Don't whimper. It didn't hurt that much. Get up!" If I gave you that speech, you would probably punch me in the nose and make me cry! But Jesus didn't hide his strong emotions: he wept at the death of his friend; he was enraged by the commercialization of the temple; he was nettled by the puny faith of his disciples.

When are athletes allowed to express their true emotions? Imagine an aging professional disclosing his anxiety about being replaced by a younger player, or a football coach talking honestly with his players about the fear of getting hurt. Because these emotions are seldom discussed, many young athletes assume that their feelings are unique and, thus, try to hide them.

Genuine self-control may be evidenced by how athletes treat opponents, referees, or erring teammates. Gilman high-school football coach Biff Poggi praised one of his players who was kicked by an opponent but didn't retaliate: "Every fiber in his body wanted to whack that guy back. But he thought of the team first. We needed him on the field more than he needed to be kicked out of the game for fighting. Now that's senior leadership!"

Aggression

The aggressive athlete gives 110 percent—straining as hard in practice as he does in games, running in situations in which others might reasonably jog, hustling in a blowout. But can that aggressive person moderate his pace? At a press conference before the 1982 Major League All-Star Game, one player suggested that "the object of the game was not about winning or losing," but rather an opportunity to "honor players who excel at their positions." Pete Rose then stepped to the podium and objected: "Losing stinks. You can't enjoy yourself unless you win."

Really Pete? Is there no difference between a World Series game and the All-Star game? Between a game of H-O-R-S-E with your son and an NCAA Tournament game? Could you enjoy a family picnic without organizing a competitive game? Could you lie on a blanket with your wife and carelessly watch leaves settle onto a glassy pond? Too often we measure the quality of life by its velocity.

Many of us parents act like our calling is to be our kids' recreation directors. We keep kids stimulated, entertained, engaged. But when will we help them develop the quiet, meditative qualities that are fundamental to Christian maturity? The Psalmist instructs us: "*When you are on your beds, search your hearts and be silent*" (4:4). But who can lie awake to do any silent searching after our exhausting schedules? The unhurried things must be nurtured.

Toughness

An athlete must be tough to be a champion. When one NFL quarterback played after he had broken a rib, his coach praised him: "It was the greatest guts job I have ever seen!"

It is good to be tough; no one likes a whiner. But if toughness is *overvalued* it may hinder the development of the vulnerability needed for relationships with God and others. The Apostle Paul proclaimed: *If I must boast, I will boast of the things that show my weakness ... so that Christ's power may rest on me.* (2 Cor. 11:30, 12:9). Paul boasted about his weaknesses because they turned him to God's strength. When was the last time you heard an athlete boast about his weaknesses?!

When Gary Warner was a high school quarterback, he spent hours working on the snap with his center: "How many snaps did Bill give me? Thousands, but I never knew Bill. Never knew what he dreamed about or hurt about or cared about." When the athletic world stresses an armor of toughness, it may discourage the humility needed to build deep, transforming friendships.

Conclusion

So what is wrong with being persistent, selfless, self-controlled, aggressive, and tough? Nothing, if properly defined. But the sportsworld's biggest problem may be what it leaves out: Where is the emphasis on *love, joy, peace, patience, kindness, and gentleness?* Jesus could be tough, driving the moneychangers from the temple. But he could also be tender—touching lepers, nestling children in his lap, accepting the kisses of a sinful woman.

But must the sportsworld teach all the values? Can't it

teach some, and homes and churches teach others? Not really.
Values are never taught in isolation. When a coach preaches
"Tenacity! Tenacity! Tenacity!" he is not simply lecturing on
the *need* for tenacity but also the *priority* of tenacity.

Jesus' priority system begins with love. An NFL Hall-of-
Famer explained that even though he and his coach shared
the same faith, they couldn't share an intimate friendship:

> *Keeping our distance was the best way to maintain a respectful*
> *coach-player dialogue. Socializing together wouldn't work*
> *because of the demands each of us faced. He had to tell me*
> *about my play, and sometimes what he had to say wasn't*
> *favorable. I had to be open with him, even if it meant saying*
> *I didn't think the last play he called was so hot.*

Is that right? Can't close friends be honest with each other?
Imagine a parent saying, "I didn't want to get too close to my
kids because I am afraid it might affect my judgment." Obviously intimacy affects our judgment, but it usually improves it!
We must think more deeply about how to make love *the* priority
in sports.

THE IDEAL JOB:
THE SPORTSWORLD AND VOCATION

> *"I loved [playing ball]. Nobody could have loved it as much*
> *as me. I must have fifty scrapbooks. Sometimes I sit by myself*
> *and take a scrapbook and just turn the pages. The hair comes*
> *up on the back of my neck. I get goose bumps. And I remember*
> *how it was and how I used to think that it would always be*

that way." — **Mickey Mantle**

Each spring, after the South Dakota winter finally melted, I played softball during my school lunch hour. As noon approached, I began to put away my books in anticipation of charging out the school door. I made a mad dash home on my bicycle, gulped down a sandwich, and dashed back to the school. With Mom's help—she had the crucial job of having lunch on the table—I could accomplish all that in under fifteen minutes, leaving forty-five minutes to play ball. During those days I dreamed, "*What could possibly be better than playing sports professionally?*" Ask a boy, "Would you rather make straight A's or be the starting quarterback on the football team?" Not many want to be the next Einstein.

Jim Bouton explained his attempt to return to the majors: "There is no use asking me why I'm here, why a reasonably intelligent thirty-year-old man who has lost his fastball is still struggling to play baseball. The dreams are the answer. They're why I wanted to be a ballplayer and why I still want to get back on top." How do we help our children develop realistic dreams? We can start by helping them understand the realities of the professionals' world.

Miniscule Numbers

Less than one million senior high boys play basketball for their school teams. By the time those same boys are seniors in college, only 15,000 still play for their school. Of those 15,000, only 200 will be drafted by professional teams, and only 50 will actually play in the NBA. Thus, the odds of a high school basketball player making it to the NBA are about 20,000 to one! When my nephew, Kyle, was a young boy, his dad tried to enlighten him about his odds of being an NBA star. Kyle took in the information and was silent for a few seconds and then asked, "Dad, do you think I'll have to spend some time in the developmental league or will I play directly in the NBA?" It may take a few reminders before the unreality of this dream takes hold!

Hard Work

It's January. I am watching the weekly PGA tournament. My mind is confused by the contrast between the warm, summery scene on my TV and the cold, icy scene outside my window. The announcer informs me that the winner will pocket one million dollars—that's more than I made in twenty years of teaching! What a life! But what I don't see is the hard work required to make it to the top: "The ideal training process means hitting about 600 balls a day. That means swinging a golf club every 45 to 60 seconds and doing it for four hours in the morning, breaking for lunch, then another four hours in the afternoon—day after day." Similarly rigorous training for swimmers led Olympian Mark Spitz to conclude: "Swimming is too demanding. It's also boring. You work six or seven hours a day just so you can splash water faster than anyone else. There's gotta be something more." (There is, Mark!)

Public Analysis

Imagine laying bare your professional life for the daily scrutiny of the national media: "We've been following the career of Professor Bernie Schock and frankly, he is quite average. He uses 'ah' and 'um' frequently. His speech is often garbled. And his illustrations are outdated. It's time for the university to find a replacement." Ridiculous? Of course, but not far from what professional athletes experience.

Though some of the analysis is based on hard statistics, much is merely opinion. Roger Federer was the Number One player in the world for over five years and had won every major title except for the French Open when one writer concluded: "No matter how many Wimbledons he wins, one title in Paris will completely change the conversation about Federer's place in the tennis hierarchy." What?! What could possibly change his place in the tennis hierarchy? He was already one of the top three or four players who had ever played. What was that loopy writer talking about?

Fans aren't much better than the media. Their attitude is "What have you done for me *today*?" One player acridly described his fans as people who would "boo funerals, an Easter egg hunt, a parade of armless vets, and the Liberty Bell." The adulation of an athlete seldom lasts longer than his skills.

Insecurity

Golf has no long-term contracts. A Major Championship on the PGA Tour gives the winner a five-year exemption from qualifying. Other winners receive only a two-year exemption. But all other golfers must finish in the top 125 on the money list to be assured a place on the next year's tour. Those who don't make the cut have to go back to Qualifying School. One golfer explained why Q-School is tougher than law school: "At least if you pass the bar, you're done. Here, you can pass the test one year and be right back taking it again the next year. And the year after and the year after." PGA golfer Mike Donald, a frequent Q-School contestant, quipped: "This isn't golf. This is combat."

Only the very top athletes receive long-term contracts. The rest must compete every year for a spot on the team. How would you like to be forced to "try out" for your job every year and know that your boss was always searching for a superior replacement? There are few professions as insecure as professional athletics.

Short Careers/Long Futures

One of my seminary professors' commencement advice was to change jobs yearly for the next ten years. Though clearly exaggerating, he believed that our greatest effectiveness was years away and that a diversity of experience would help us discover and refine our gifts. But a professional athlete's best years are in his twenties or thirties. Tennis star Jennifer Capriati became a professional when she was thirteen-years-old! But when injuries ended her career, she worried about what she would do for the next fifty years. Those fears led to an emotional breakdown: "When I stopped playing, that's when all this came crumbling down... I can't live off of [my past] the rest of my life." All athletes must eventually retire; the average professional career lasts only three or four years. Then an athlete faces the challenge of filling his life with purposeful work.

Family Life

In his book, *Whenever I Wind Up* Cy Young award winner (2012) RA Dickey reported that his job as a major leaguer heaped a lopsided burden on his wife:

> *When you are away so much, almost every conversation back home seems to be conducted in a pressure cooker, where you talk about new tires for the car, kids' ear infections, and the swelling cell phone bill, all in rapid order.*
>
> *If you have any self-awareness at all, you realize how uneven the distribution of responsibilities is. Your wife is going to the pediatrician and calling the plumber and meeting with the teacher, and you are working on your knuckleball grip in a bullpen session.*
>
> *Your wife is reading bedtime stories and checking for monsters in the closet and then getting up first thing for school, while you are hanging out with the guys after a game and sleeping until 11 in the morning.*

Similarly, professional golfer Paul Azinger was always conflicted between his need to be at home as a father, and on the road as a golfer. He explained that the most difficult part of leaving was hearing a child plead, "Daddy, please don't go; please don't go."

Some athletes make heroic choices to care for their families. When Danny Ainge quit as the head coach of the NBA's Phoenix Suns, he explained: "I love coaching, but anyone can coach. My wife has just one husband and my children have just one father. Some of you may think I'm jumping ship. I don't believe I'm jumping ship. I'm diving overboard to save my family." Yea, Danny Ainge!

No Satisfaction

After Roger Federer lost the U.S. Open Final in 2009, he congratulated the winner, Juan Del Potro. Then he reminded the national audience that "I had a great tournament myself." Though Del Potro "was the best," he said, "I've had an unbelievable run here. I never thought five or six years ago that I would win forty matches in a row. It's been an amazing run for me." Why did he spend most of his concession speech talking about his own accomplishments? Because, as one superstar recognized, athletic success never fully delivers: "Reaching one peak is never sufficient. We will always need more kudos and more championships to feel content."

Conclusion

The dream of professional athletics has captured the hearts of many of our young people. Our challenge as Christian parents is to build into our kids the infinitely higher dream of serving the Eternal God: *Seek first his kingdom and his righteousness, and all these things will be given to you as well.* (Matt. 6:33) Building this vision will be the subject of the next chapter.

CHAPTER EIGHT

Parents as Models

"We have seen the enemy and he is us."

— **Pogo**

"An interest can become a hobby;
a hobby can become a passion;
a passion can become an obsession."

— **Unknown**

Richard Lipsky attended track meets with his dad during his youth. Lipsky, in *How We Play the Game,* observed: "[Dad's] whole world of meaning and triumph was re-created before his eyes, as well as mine. He would point out the different strides of the runners, talk excitedly about finishing kicks, and come alive—be happy—in ways I never otherwise saw. *I could not have received a more vivid lesson about what is important in life"* (emphasis mine). Mr. Lipsky was a teacher. Oh, he didn't have a syllabus or quizzes or required texts; nevertheless, he effectively communicated his passion to his son.

As Christians, we hope to impart "vivid lessons" about what is *eternally* important to our children. We do this by our walk (modeling):

> *Love the Lord your God with all your heart and with all your soul and with all your strength. These commandments that I give you today must be on your hearts. (Deuteronomy 6:5-6)*

...And our talk (teaching):

> *Impress [these commandments] on your children. Talk about them when you sit at home and when you walk along the road, when you lie down and when you get up. Tie them as symbols on your hands and bind them on your foreheads. Write them on the doorframes of your houses and on your gates. (6:7-9)*

This chapter focuses on the walking, and the next on the talking. You can't pass on what you don't possess. If God isn't your passion, then he isn't likely to be your child's passion.

Parents' Passions

One New York Giants fan recounted the celebration that erupted when the final whistle blew and the Giants won the 2008 Super Bowl. He was "surrounded by delirious Giants fans who were hugging and screaming and crying and acting like stranded castaways who just noticed a rescue boat." Furthermore, in the state of Texas, high-school football is "discussed in churches, cafes, schools, Kiwanis club meetings, oil fields, and out on the north forty.

Football, particularly high-school football, is the staff of life." As I have said earlier, the sportsworld was my god. It was my "staff of life," filling my days and my dreams and my desires. When I became a Christian, I was confronted with the truth that I could not serve two masters. I could worship God or my alternate god—but not both. God won't share his throne.

Parents, your primary call in life is to fervently love God: *Love the Lord your God with all your heart and with all your soul and with all your strength. These commandments I give you today are to be upon your hearts.* (Deut. 6:5-6) When I have counseled parents that it is okay to occasionally miss their children's sporting events, some look at me as if I am advocating child sacrifice! But if your relationship with God is the priority of your life, won't you need to occasionally miss a child's ball game to attend a retreat or a home Bible study? If you always sacrifice those activities for your child's athletics, what are you teaching your child? You can build your life around God or around your child's sporting life—but you can't do both.

A number of years ago, I asked my wife to record a championship football game for me because I had another commitment. Because I enjoy the unexpected in sports, I made it clear to my sons that I wanted to view the game without knowing the final score. When I came home, my six year-old son greeted me with "Dad, I won't tell you the score but I don't think you will want to watch it." I immediately knew that my team had lost. I responded sharply, "Andrew, you weren't supposed to tell me!" Unfortunately, my values were showing.

I was more concerned about a trivial football game than my treasured son.

Though we can still enjoy sports, the challenge for many of us is to become more temperate about them. C.S. Lewis, in *Mere Christianity*, defines temperance as "going the right length and no further" with our pleasures. Though temperance has been narrowly applied to drinking alcohol, it should apply to any of our pleasures. If I make golf or the Minnesota Twins or my child's athletics the center of my life, I am being "just as intemperate as someone who gets drunk every evening. Of course, it does not show on the outside so easily: golf-mania does not make you fall down in the middle of the road. *But God is not deceived by externals*" (emphasis mine). Lewis believes that God judges a sports obsession just as negatively as he does an alcohol obsession. In both cases, I am under the control of something other than God.

When sports are an idol for parents, they may try to serve that idol through their children. One father explained that watching his son play football "was almost like I was competing myself again." Ouch! Parents, please understand; your childhood is over and your child still has his to live! Appointing your children to fulfill your dreams puts a burden on them that they are too young to bear or comprehend.

Modeling Godly Passions

The Ark of the Covenant, the gold-covered chest that housed the tablets of the Law and the presence of God, was the most holy item in Israel's worship. Not long after the Philistines captured it, David restored it to his people. During the ark's homecoming celebration, David *danced before the Lord with all his might ... leaping and dancing before the Lord.* (II Sam. 6:16) He was so unrestrained that his wife, Michal, was embarrassed and called him a *vulgar fellow!* But David was resolute: *I will celebrate before the Lord. And I will become even more undignified than this* (II Sam. 6:21).

Where do people today become so "undignified"? While attending a high school football game, H.G. Bissinger heard "deep-throated yells, violent exhortations, giddy screams, hoarse whoops. The people in the stands lost all sight of who they were and what they were supposed to be like, all dignity and restraint thrown aside because of these high-school boys in front of them, their boys, their heroes." Doesn't that sound like David? They "lost all sight of who they were and what they were supposed to be like, all dignity and restraint thrown aside" (*Friday Night Lights*).

We must think clearly and creatively about how we can model a whole-hearted love for God to our children. What do you model when you attend a worship service? Are you reluctant to shout an "Amen!" or raise your hands in praise? You may decline, claiming that you aren't a demonstrative person. But didn't I see you throw your arms in the air and hear you scream, "Touchdown!!" during last week's NFL game?

Though my boys saw my passion for the sportsworld, they also saw my passion for the spiritual world. During our family's Easter celebrations we played David Meece's resurrection song, "Today Is the Day," repeatedly and loudly. That energetic song became a staple of our Easter traditions as we sang and marched around the house, rejoicing in our risen Savior. May God increase our freedom to love Him with our whole selves.

Removing Idols

Sports are a significant part of our daily lives. Consider the statistics:

- 88% of kids (ages 8-17) watch televised sports.

- 75% of all Americans watch sports weekly.

- 70% of adults read about, discuss, or participate in sports *daily*.

But when a sports hobby becomes a sports obsession, people (like me!) become enslaved. Since the way to break free from an addiction is to starve it, I had to cut myself off from excessive sports information. For many years I did not subscribe to cable television or the daily newspaper. I also turned down a long-standing offer from my father to purchase a satellite TV system for our family. I made these choices because I wanted to limit the daily temptations to indulge in sports. Today, I infrequently use my computer to chase down sports statistics and rarely watch ESPN's *Sports Center*, because both feed my craving.

Televised sports try to hook us with the illusion that outcomes are critical. Thus, the Game of the Week is hyped as the Game of the Century. When Michigan State's basketball team qualified to play in the 2009 NCAA championship game, and that game was to be played in economically depressed Detroit, much was written about what a great boost it was to the state. But what difference did it actually make in the lives of Michigan residents? Was their economic or emotional plight any different a day later? A month later? A year later? How was that game more than a temporary diversion from their struggles?

I bought into the myth that results matter. Therefore, the games took precedence over people and other responsibilities. But a strange thing happened when I adopted God's perspective—that results are relatively unimportant, that success and winning are not the same, that I won't care who won a week from now, that failure is good for athletes, etc., etc. When I engaged in this self-talk, I found my zeal subsiding. It didn't happen all at once; I had to persist with this self-talk. But I now find that sports often bore me. Today I am more interested in a close game, excellent play, and good sportsmanship than in seeing my team win. When I hear announcers trumpet the magnitude of a game, I chuckle and remind myself that it is truly just a game. As one Super Bowl participant insightfully observed, "If this was the ultimate game, they wouldn't be playing it again next year."

I have other strategies to help me control my addiction. For example, I avoid watching most televised events from start to finish, often tuning in past the middle of the game. If the game is a blowout, I don't waste time on it. I also mute the sound on many events so that I can perform other tasks—sorting through a closet, paying bills, grading papers, answering e-mails, reading a magazine, etc.

Finally, and most importantly, I am less attracted to my alternate God when I practice the priority of loving God more through study, prayer, fellowship, and worship. As the Apostle Peter wrote: *Like newborn babies, crave pure spiritual milk... now that you have tasted that the Lord is good.* (I Pet. 2:2,3) As I tasted the sweetness of my God, sports soured in comparison.

Athletes As Role Models

I was an NBA all-star year after year. The arena in which I achieved that feat was my driveway! I imagined playing as a prized teammate of my beloved Boston Celtics. Even with Bill Russell and Bob Cousy on my team, I always made the last-second shot, the critical steal, or the amazing block that secured another championship for the world's best basketball team.

My driveway fantasies were not unique. All children emulate others in their play. When children imitate a princess or a superhero or an NBA star, they are "putting on" the clothing of adult life. We are designed for imitation. The Bible is filled with exhortations to imitate God: *Be holy as I am holy.* (Lev. 19:2) The Apostle Paul asked his disciples to imitate him. Because imitation is one of the pathways to maturity, children need role models who are worth emulating. Sadly, today's sportsworld heroes often fall short because "our generation has lowered the standards and amped up the volume."

Character or Characters?

Today's sports media often fixate on some of sports' most tarnished models. When baseball star Manny Ramirez was suspended for 50 games for steroid use, the media followed his play in minor-league games (Why was he allowed to play anywhere?), updated the progress of his suspension, and then showcased his performance when he returned. Does this help young athletes stay clean? In today's sportsworld, all that an athlete needs is a high level of achievement and he will be "elevated to icon status." His character seldom matters.

But God is more concerned about character than achievement. The Apostle Paul instructed Timothy to *set an example for the believers in speech, in life, in love, in faith, and in purity.* Though he had work to do (*devote yourself to preaching and teaching*), he was warned to monitor his life: *Watch your life and doctrine closely. Persevere in them, because if you do, you will save both yourself and your hearers.* His character was the basis for his impact (I Tim. 4:12-16).

Juan Pierre was a lifetime .300 hitter before he signed with the Los Angeles Dodgers. During his first year as a Dodger, he played in all 162 games, as he had done for the previous four years. But the next year Pierre was benched. He didn't handle the demotion well. One of the sportswriters described him as "sullen" and "almost sad." But the next year he returned to the Dodgers with a new attitude. Though the Dodgers' addition of free agents decreased his likelihood of playing regularly, he was determined to return a new man: "I wasn't happy with myself last year. I have always read the Bible, but I was reading it again during the off-season.... I just figured out God's plan is way better than mine. I thought I could do it on my own, but I was miserable. I can only control things that I can control. "Players and media noticed the difference. One sports writer observed that in such a refreshing way, nothing seems to unsettle him." His peace was based on the belief that God is in control. Our athletic kids will face adversity in their sports: riding the bench, injuries, unjust umpiring, incompetent coaches. Athletes like Pierre can model how to handle these uncontrollable and unwelcome events.

Parents often ask "Should I shield my kids from athletes who are drug addicts or adulterers or egomaniacs?" Not necessarily. The Bible doesn't edit out the sins of its heroes. Jacob was a schemer, Moses a murderer, Samson a fornicator, and David an adulterer and a murderer. The Bible presents both the good and the bad because we learn from both. The exposure of Tiger Woods's sexual addiction and his ensuing problems on and off the golf course can be a "good" model for children, shouting the truth that a man reaps what he sows.

Other Heroes

At some point nearly all kids recognize that they won't mimic their sports hero's accomplishments. This won't frustrate them if their definition of a hero emphasizes character over achievement; then *all* kids can become heroes. A true hero is not the star athlete who plays ball for millions and before millions, but rather a mother who selflessly teaches her handicapped child how to care for herself. It is not the athlete who produces the clutch hit but rather an aging, pain-ridden husband who cares compassionately for his bed-ridden wife.

Kids used to have more realistic dreams; they hoped to be a teacher or a missionary or an inventor. They still need that exposure to these genuine heroes. Be creative. Take a family vacation to the mission field. Find a mature Christian who will allow your child to be his apprentice for the summer. Read books about Christian heroes like William Wilberforce or Adoniram Judson. As author Dick Keyes points out, such heroes challenge the "mediocrity of our lives and open us to new possibilities of what we might become."

No Perfect Models

As my son Jered's soccer team prepared for the final tournament in their final season, I was pleased with our draw; the two best teams were in the other division and we were favored in ours. I envisioned a storybook ending for the team, winning our division and then upsetting the winner of the other division. One of the reasons why I coached was to provide a model of Christian maturity to my sons, their teammates, and their parents. And since the games took place in our hometown, a victory would also model to other local teams that you can win with a players-first philosophy.

But fantasy seldom predicts reality. In the closing minute of our first game, the referee (who was forty yards out of position) whistled us for a foul, awarding our opponent a penalty kick, which they made. The referee clearly made the wrong call, with the game ending in a 1-1 tie. I was very upset, yelling repeatedly: "That's the worst call I have ever seen!"

In our second game, we played a strong first half and led 2-0. But officiating errors and sloppy play led to a three-to-two loss. On one occasion, I angrily slammed my hat to the ground and stomped on it to protest a call. (Why does any sane man stomp on his own hat?) In our final game, in which we faced our toughest opponent, we were playing exceptional soccer and leading four to nothing at halftime. I thought, "*Well, at least we'll go out on a high note.*" But the second half was a disaster. We were badly outplayed, and our goalkeeper made two phenomenal saves to preserve a four-to-four tie. And just before the final whistle, a first-ever fistfight broke out between my team and our opponents. Had my temper fueled their fists?

As I went home that evening I was very disappointed in myself; what a pathetic model of Christian maturity! But before I worked myself into a funk over my coaching failure, I reflected on the past seven years. I had grown in my ability to love and lead young men, to control my volatile emotions, to trust God with their performance, to applaud the excellent play of an opponent, etc. Thankfully, God is looking for *progress, not perfection*, in his models.

Conclusion

My sons' athletics were a tool that God used to refine me. Because sports had been my childhood lifeline, I battled repeatedly to see my sons' athletics in the light of God's truth. During one difficult time, I confessed in my journal: "In my mind, I know that God is in control and I know my son will have the experience that God wants him and us to have. But I'm tired of fighting this battle, Lord. I won't be disappointed when their youth sports will be completed and I no longer have to fight this battle." God was working on me, rooting out the god of the sportsworld from the recesses of my heart. God was transforming my life so that he could use me to help transform others' lives.

CHAPTER NINE

Parents as Teachers

"When we worry about our children liking us, we put our needs ahead of our children's needs."

**— David Elkind, Child Psychologist
& Author**

"Our problems in life don't stem from loving ourselves too little, but of loving others and God too little."

—Leslie Vernick, Biblical Counselor

When I was ten years old and my cousin was thirteen, we traveled with my family to Chicago, where we attended our first major-league baseball game. I had watched games on TV, but the cameras edited out the richness of the ballpark. I was awed by Wrigley Field: the grass was lush and perfectly clipped; the outfield walls were covered with an emerald-green ivy; the infield was smooth and finely textured—unlike the rock-infested field on which I played; the foul lines were the whitest and straightest that I had ever seen. I treasured the sounds—the loud pop of the catcher's mitt, the rifle-shot crack of the bat, the roar of the crowd, the bellow of the home-plate umpire, the bark of food vendors ("Get your red-hot hot dogs!"). I marveled at the infielders' handling of "routine" ground balls. I was astonished by the rocketing fly balls that seemed to touch the clouds. I scrambled after foul balls, hoping to retrieve a gen-u-ine, major-league baseball. My cousin and I were so dazzled by the spectacle that we cajoled my parents into letting us return the next day on our own. (That wouldn't happen in today's riskier world!) Such experiences led me to become a passionate disciple of baseball, and ultimately, of the whole sportsworld.

When the sportsworld offers such compelling experiences, how can we parents hope to guide our children toward becoming disciples of Jesus Christ? Though the sportsworld does an extraordinary job of making disciples, Christians can do better. But we must think clearly and soberly about what a child needs to know and experience to become a full disciple of Jesus.

The Priority of Love

Jesus made it clear: there is nothing more important than developing a whole-hearted love for God and your neighbor (Mark. 12:28-30). And the Apostle Paul claimed that without love we are *nothing*. (1 Cor. 13:1-3). Dick Keyes in his book, *True Heroism,* explains:

> *No matter how spectacular, gifted, or dedicated a person*
> *might be, without love it is all ashes at God's feet. No matter*
> *how much else I have or do, it comes to nothing without love.*
> *It is much like multiplying by zero in mathematics. No matter*
> *how large a number we multiply by zero, the result is always*
> *the same—zero.*

But what priority do we parents give to raising lovers? Psychologist Polly Young-Eisendrath has written, "instead of helping our children learn how to work, love, and share... we have taught them to focus on their own achievement." Be honest: Would you rather have a son who is an All-State quarterback or a young man who mentors younger boys? Would you rather have a child who is the valedictorian of her class or a child whose friends turn to her for advice and support?

Though it isn't always an either/or choice, training our children to love must take precedence over *anything* else.

Loving God

Ryan Hall holds the American-born record in the marathon (2:06:17) and the half-marathon (59:43). As I wrote earlier, he almost quit his sport, but found his way back to running by revitalizing his relationship with God. FCA's *Sharing the Victory* explained that instead of "living, sleeping, eating and breathing to be the best runner in the world, he had to learn to live, sleep, eat and breathe Christ above all."

The challenge for Christian parents is how to help our kids "live, sleep, eat and breathe Christ above all." We tried to do this by helping our boys see their competition through God's eyes. When Nathan was playing collegiate soccer and struggling with a lack of recognition from his coach (even though he was the second-leading scorer on the team), I wrote to him:

> *How is the ankle? I believe those weak ankles were given to you by God to keep you humble! The lack of recognition you have received from your coach is also God-designed. I frequently counsel troubled people who are looking for recognition, approval, or love from someone who can't or won't give as much as the person thinks he needs. Nathan, if you learn to seek God's approval first, and not be overly concerned about the approval of others, it will provide a stable foundation to weather the storms of life.*
>
> *God judges by a different standard than the world does. The world will cheer if you score goals. God will cheer if you comfort a teammate who is discouraged by his playing time. The world will cheer if you lead your team to a championship. God will cheer if you maintain a gracious attitude toward a horrible referee. The world will cheer if you dedicate everything you have to becoming a better soccer player. God will cheer if you discipline yourself to spend time with Him: "Physical training is of some value, but godliness has value for all things, holding promise for both the present life and the life to come." (I Tim. 4:8).*

There were more critical issues in my son's life than coaches' approval or sprained ankles or playing time or goals scored. I wanted him to see that a loving God was molding and shaping his life through his athletic trials.

As parents, we need to steer our kids toward activities that nurture a love for God. Unfortunately, many parents say that they want their children to love God, but allow sports to fill their kids' summers. The kids don't attend church camp— instead they take part in two or three sports camps. The kids don't participate in a mission trip—instead they compete in a baseball tournament that week. Parents defend these choices by claiming that their hands are tied by coaches' threats of lost playing time or even a spot on the team. But even if those threats materialize, which they seldom do, did Jesus ever say that following him wouldn't involve sacrifice?

Loving in the Sportsworld

Love is not highly valued in the sportsworld. When Billy Donovan led Florida to back-to-back NCAA basketball championships, sportswriter Dan Wetzel wrote about Florida's coach: "He is likeable, yes. But loveable? Well, who cares? Loveable would never have gotten back to [the championship game]." Wetzel and many others believe that being loveable would prevent a coach from being able to build championship teams because there "is always more important work to do." More important than what? What could be more important for a coach than to love his players and teach them how to love?

Not all in the sportsworld make love a detrimental or dispensable commodity. Joe Ehrmann and "Biff" Poggi coach the Gilman High School football team, which has often been rated among the country's best. Their winning philosophy is grounded in love. They explain their priorities in one of the season's first team meetings:

"What is our job?" Biff asked.

"To love us," most of the boys yelled back.

"And what is your job?" Biff shouted back.

"To love each other," the boys responded.

Ehrmann and Poggi have found that emphasizing love has not hurt their team's achievement and it serves the boys well outside of football.

We need to be creative in teaching the priority of love to our athletic children. Here are some possibilities:

- Your talented child might invite a less-talented teammate to practice with her.

- An older child could volunteer to help coach younger kids.

- Help your child learn how to recognize and love the various personality types on his team: the bossy, the discouraged, the lazy, the egotistical, the talented, the untalented, the complainers, etc.

- Be careful as to what you praise. After a winning baseball game, you might praise your son's grace under pressure: "Son, I was impressed that you didn't make an ugly face when the ump called you out on that worm-level pitch."

Loving in the Everyday World

Psychologist John Rosemond believes that children need self-respect more than self-esteem. Self-respect is based on the "knowledge that you are making a positive contribution.... A person with self-respect focuses primarily on his or her obligations to *others*." These obligations begin in the home where families can teach love's basics:

- Serving ("I need you to play with your little sister while I make dinner.")

- Resolving conflicts ("I always have to wash dishes!")

- Engaging in teamwork ("Let's all weed the garden and then we can go for a bike ride.")

Journalist Regan McMahon believes that mealtimes are a critical component in this educational process: "I'm ready to draw a line in the tablecloth. Eating together is the cornerstone of family life, the ritual that nourishes us in more ways than one, it is the time kids learn manners, learn to listen to their siblings, and absorb adult vocabulary and ideas." Research confirms her praise: "The more often a child eats dinner with his or her family, the less likely that child is to smoke, drink, or use illegal drugs."

Parents, *preteen* children need you to control decisions about family time. One fall, two of our boys missed a championship soccer game because it conflicted with a previously planned family vacation. Though they would have chosen to stay, we decided that the trip was more important.

But by the time kids reach their *middle teens* they should make more of these decisions. One December when two of our boys were playing high-school basketball, they had a tough choice to make. Our extended family has a holiday tradition of traveling to the Twin Cities to shop for presents and hang out together. The boys had it worked out with their coach— we would drive to the Cities after their Saturday night game and stay over Sunday night, returning to Sioux Falls in time for afternoon classes and practice. But the coach unexpectedly changed practice to Monday morning. If they missed, they would lose playing time in the next game. They both decided to stick with the family tradition and suffer the consequences. Yea! Our boys were coming to understand the relative importance of athletics.

Children's Identity

As I have explained, one of my childhood goals was to play basketball for Sioux Falls' one public high school (of 3000 students!). My dedication to that goal included an extra hour or two of practice each day during the basketball season. When I was unexpectedly cut during my senior year, I was devastated because my identity was based on basketball.

Similarly, when tennis star Jennifer Capriati lost her job because of injuries, she agonized over the void that it created: "If I don't have [tennis], who am I? What am I? I was just alive because of this. I've had to ask, 'Well, who is Jennifer? What if this is gone now?'" She wondered: "How am I going to live on this earth and wake up happy with who I am?" She had defined herself solely by her tennis.

Building a Stable Identity

Many parents believe that building a child's self-esteem is the basis for a sturdy identity. But neither contemporary research nor the Bible affirms that children benefit from high self-esteem. Psychologist John Rosemond reports, in his book *Parenting by the Book,* that research has found that children who measure high in self-esteem demonstrate lower "self-control, especially when they aren't getting their way. They don't handle defeat or disappointment very well. Why? Because people with high self-esteem think they are entitled to always be the winner."

The Scriptures uniformly condemn *high* self-esteem. In the beatitudes Jesus praised those who are *poor in spirit.* Peter informs us that God *opposes the proud but shows favor to the humble.* So the goal for our kids is low self-esteem? No. The Apostle Paul believed that there was a middle ground: "Do not think of yourself more highly than you ought. (Rom. 12:3)" In other words, don't think too highly or too lowly of yourself. Though low self-esteem can be a problem, the Biblical remedy is not high self-esteem; it is humility, modesty, and meekness.

Our children will have a healthy identity when they embrace their God-based identity. This includes:

- Their creation by a loving God — *You created my inmost being; you knit me together in my mother's womb; I praise you because I am fearfully and wonderfully made.* (Ps.139:13)

- Their salvation through Christ's sacrifice — *God demonstrates his own love for us in this: While we were yet sinners, Christ died for us.* (Rom. 5:8)

- Their participation in the body of Christ — *Now to each one the manifestation of the Spirit is given for the common good.* (I Cor. 12:7)

Satan attacked Jesus' identity: "If you are really the Son of God..." (Matt. 4:3) Do you hear the sarcasm? Similarly, the Serpent will seek to poison your child's identity. After an extended losing streak, a coach might scream: "You guys are a bunch of losers! You'll never amount to anything!" God's truth is the only antidote to such venom: "You are God's son and Christ's brother!"

Though more than one hundred boys tried out for my high school's sophomore basketball team, only thirty made the team. By the time we were seniors, only ten made the varsity team. Only one of those ten played in college. As children age, more and more are excluded from athletic teams. But the exclusions are also experienced elsewhere. Only a few kids win scholarships. Only a handful become homecoming kings and queens. Only a few win the leads in school plays. However, in God's world no one is excluded; *all* are needed, *all* are gifted, *all* have assigned tasks. In fact, the Apostle Paul said that those who *seem to be weaker, are indispensable!* (I Cor.12:22). What a blessing! A child who understands his *inclusion* in God's world won't be blown away by the world's *exclusions.* We are partners with the Ruler of the Universe!

Unfortunately, some parents try to shape their child into

the person whom they want her to be. Dr. Roni Cohen-Sandler, who has investigated the lives of stressed-out girls, has found that many girls are "busy living up to others' expectations." They are "so focused on achieving success that they don't get the chance to figure out what really excites them and gives them pleasure. They barely know who they are or who they want to become." How sad. Children who pursue others' designs for their lives may become alienated from their creator's design for them.

Our kids need a diversity of experiences to help them find their niche in God's world—participation in service projects, caring for young children, spending time with God, attending church camps, volunteering in the community, relating to grandparents, holding a job, teaching at Vacation Bible School. Such a variety of experience will help kids discover how God has uniquely gifted them.

The Identity of Boys

Joe Ehrmann explained the significance of athletic achievement for boys: "If you can hit the hanging curve in baseball or catch the down-and-out pass in football, then you immediately get elevated as being a little more masculine, a little bit better than the other boys."

Boys are graded more by what happens on the playing field than what happens in the classroom. A former head coach at a major southern university echoed this sentiment when he claimed that boys growing up in the South "have to play football to be accepted as a man." Ouch! If athletic achievement is the only way in which boys can establish their masculinity, many, many boys will struggle. Too often these boys who fail on the playing fields are made to feel like failures in life.

Some coaches exploit the manhood-through-sports myth to get a maximum effort out of their athletes. One former college star believed that his coach played on the players' "fears of masculinity, fears of acceptance, fears of not being good enough.... We were trying to prove ourselves as men and we wanted approval from an authority that we'd passed the test." Similarly, Ehrmann believes that a dysfunctional father-son relationship drove many of his former teammates—they played to earn a father's approval.

When athletics is the road to acceptance as a man, both "losers" and "winners" are losers. One college star confessed: "For us to believe in this system of male winners made it practically impossible not to think of ourselves as .... superior, real men." We should be concerned when sports produce broken losers or haughty winners.

But how should boys be measured? What is the meaning of manhood? As discussed above, it revolves around their ability to love. Ehrmann believes masculinity ought to be taught in terms of the capacity to love and to be loved. If you look over your life at the end of it, life wouldn't be measured in what you've acquired or achieved or what you own. It's going to come down to this:

1. **What kind of father were you?**
2. **What kind of husband were you?**

3. **What kind of coach or teammate were you?**
4. **What kind of son were you?**
5. **What kind of brother were you?**
6. **What kind of friend were you?**

Some athletes understand their true identity. When people wondered why former MVP quarterback Kurt Warner wasn't more impressed by his own accomplishments, he explained: "People think that whatever happens on the football field should define me one way or the other, but it's like, whatever.... It just happens to be what I do. *I want to be defined by what I believe in, by who I am.*" Kurt Warner's healthy identity will endure long after football.

Passing on the Faith

One young football star explained the pain he experienced after his high school career ended: "You just can't let somethin' like that go. It's like you're married for thirty years and all of a sudden you get a divorce. You don't just stop lovin' somethin.' You just don't give the better part of your life away and just stop thinkin' about it ... I want to play football bad. There isn't a day I don't think about it. There isn't an hour."

How can we parents compete with such powerful experiences? Our primary resource is God's Truth. Parents are instructed to *impress [these commands] on your children when you sit at home and when you walk along the road, when you lie down and when you get up.* (Deut. 6:7) One study found that 60% of men and 40% of women talk frequently or very frequently about sports. I wonder; what percentage of Christian parents talk frequently, or very frequently, about spiritual matters? We must learn how to surround our kids with conversation about what is supremely important.

Observing Sports with Your Children

Since many of our children regularly watch televised sports, watching with them provides great opportunities to talk about God's Truth. After watching an NCAA Championship basketball game which ended when a player threw the ball to an opponent who then scored the winning basket, I asked my boys which player I would have been most proud to call my son. They were unsure. I said that it wasn't the highest scorer or the best defender. It was the player who wrapped his consoling arms around his erring teammate at the end of the game.

Many sporting events cry out for a divine perspective. Consider the case of Mike Houck. Wrestler Houck twice attempted to qualify to represent the U.S. at the Olympic Games. In the finals at the 1984 Olympic Trials, he and Steve Fraser competed in a best-of-three Wrestle-Off. Fraser won the first. Houck won the second. They tied three to three in the third. But a tie-breaking procedure gave Fraser the Olympic berth. Fraser then won the gold at the 1984 Games. Houck came so close that he decided to train for another four years for a shot at the 1988 team. Once again he made the finals but lost the tie-breaking third match 10-9! Not surprisingly, he moaned: "It's an intense disappointment."

Now, how would you talk about Houck's failures with your child?

- Do you think Houck has any regrets?

- How would God want Houck to evaluate his experience?

- How do spiritual rewards compare to earthly rewards?

- Should an athlete work this long and hard to try to qualify for the Olympics?

Such questions may help your child begin to see life's disappointments through God's eyes.

Many of the opportunities to cultivate our kids' love for God come unexpectedly. One high-school football player gushed about playing before 20,000 fans in a championship game: "Man, that's a high no drug or booze or woman can give you." Consider the questions you might ask your kids:

- Does God give "highs"? How do they compare to athletic "highs"?

- What sort of rewards are there for serving God? Who will enjoy these rewards?

- What would it be like to stand before heaven's multitudes and hear Jesus proclaim: "Well done, good and faithful servant"?

This boy's praise for athletic pursuits could be an opportunity to help our children to understand which rewards endure. One former NBA player understands this: "There is a truth I now understand. When everything is said and done, all I will be is the answer to a trivia question."

Observing Children's Growth

It will take time to know if your pupils are learning their lessons. After Nathan was unexpectedly cut from his college soccer team after two seasons as a starter, he wrote: "I think God's response to this recent absence of athletics in my life is: 'Finally!' Ever since 8th grade I believe God has been trying to teach me personally the lesson in I Tim. 4:8: *For physical training is of some value, but godliness has value for all things, holding promise for both the present life and the life to come.* I believe that God has repeatedly put obstacles, primarily in the form of injuries and coaches, in my athletic career in order to humble me and make me realize their relative insignificance to Christ and his Kingdom." "Hallelujah!" Our son was learning what is foremost in life. When a child begins to understand that the fullest, most rewarding life is found in the Living God, he won't be enticed by other gods.

CHAPTER TEN

Christians in the Sportsworld

"Texas football is an 'immense tradition where winning football games is a sacrament of such emotional intensity as to rival those of any other religion.'"

—Gary Shaw, A Former Texas Player

Our son Nathan played on a top-ranked soccer team at a Christian university. During his first three years he was the second leading scorer and a consistent starter. But during the preseason of his senior year he was curtly cut from the team, the coach simply explaining that he wasn't in shape.

After we and our son stopped fuming and started praying, the three of us asked for a meeting with the coach and the athletic director (AD). In that meeting, I explained that Cathy and I didn't object to Nathan's release from the team; a college coach should control that issue. But what we objected to was *how* he had been cut. Why didn't a Christian coach ask why he wasn't in top condition? (A badly sprained ankle during the summer had retarded his training.) Why wouldn't he thank a boy for his dedication over the past three years? Why wouldn't he express concern for how this blow would impact a young man? Though a secular school might be expected to act this way, shouldn't a Christian university have a higher standard? (Several of Nathan's *non-Christian* friends made that observation!) During the interview we discovered that these student-athletes had no official way to evaluate their coaches, even though all of their classroom experiences included student evaluations. For the sake of future athletes in these programs, we suggested that the AD develop a similar means of evaluating the school's sports programs.

All Christians in sport must seriously ask: Are we reflecting the values of our culture or the values of Christ's kingdom? Although Christian involvement in sports is flourishing, is our impact also thriving?

THE INFLUENCED? OR THE INFLUENCERS?

Emphasis on Winning

One Christian leader explained that winning provides Christians with a megaphone to the world: "Who has better attendance—first-place or last-place teams? Who is featured in the newspapers more—the nation's finest or the also-rans? Who do people write about, talk about, pay to see? Winners!" So if I coach at a Christian university and want to win as a testimony to others, what priority will winning take? If winning is too highly valued, I may ignore my players' need for guidance in their daily lives; I may come to view the school's athletic mission as its most important task; I may recruit players who help win games but don't exhibit Christian character. Winning can be *a* goal but it can never be *the* goal.

Athletes' Testimonials

If LeBron James can be used to sell athletic shoes, shouldn't Christian athletes be used to "sell" Jesus? This common practice sounds reasonable. (My college fellowship developed a similar strategy of evangelizing campus leaders, believing that they would have the greatest impact on others.) But where is the biblical justification for using the strong to reach the weak? Did the early church recruit the wealthy, government officials or religious leaders to proclaim the Gospel? Not at all. Paul claimed that *God chose the foolish things of the world to shame the wise; God chose the weak things of the world to shame the strong. He chose the lowly things of this world and the despised things—and the things that are not—to nullify the things that are, so that no one may boast before him.* (1 Cor. 1:27-29) God wants to use "nobodies" to humble and reach the "somebodies."

Unfortunately, when Christians in sport trumpet the strong, kids may be more prone to pursue the uncertain glory of the sportsworld rather than the certain glory of God's kingdom. Might it be better to showcase a "nobody"—an injured reserve or the backup quarterback or the coach who was just fired? Is it possible that Heisman Trophy winner Tim Tebow, after being cut from the NFL, may have a greater impact as he models how to deal with life's everyday disappointments?

The Fellowship of Christian Athletes has demonstrated a refreshing balance in who they lift up as sports heroes. In their magazine *Sharing the Victory* (STV), they often carry articles on both "winners" and "losers." One issue featured the struggles of pitcher Russ Ortiz (who has won over 100 major-league games). When Ortiz first became injured, he began with a good attitude: "This stinks but God obviously has a reason, so I'm okay with it." But when he didn't heal quickly, his attitude tanked. At that low point, God began to teach him vital lessons: "I learned more than I had in my entire life. Once the injury hit, I got off God's main road and started going down my own path. Then I kept making turns, but they were all taking me away from the main road. I was getting lost and confused and mad and impatient, but I didn't care to ask God for directions." Ortiz concluded: "I didn't just go through this so I could get back to playing baseball. I came out of this trial so I could grow closer to God." Wow! That's a message kids need to hear. Would they hear it from a "winner"?

When we use celebrated athletes to proclaim Christ, do we choose them for their athletic or their spiritual achievements? When a well-known and successful Christian coach, who is also a husband and father, works twenty-hour days during the athletic season, sometimes sleeping at his office, what sort of a model is that for other husbands and fathers? Why don't we lovingly confront this brother with his out-of-balance lifestyle, rather than invite him to speak at our athletic banquets?

Finally, using winning athletes to promote Jesus may also be dangerous for these victors. Many are young in their faith and need more private nurturing than public testifying to build that faith. Paul's injunction to not appoint a new believer to be a leader may apply here. We must be careful not to abuse these "rookies" in the faith or *"they may become conceited and fall under the same judgment as the devil"* (1 Tim. 3:6).

Athletes' Commitments

One Christian leader in the sportsworld gave this advice to Christian athletes: "Your athletic abilities have been given to you by God. You have more than some athletes and less than others.... God expects you to invest wisely the talents you do have." This is sound advice—up to a point. The problem is that dedication to athletic talents often trumps other God-given talents and commitments. One world-class Christian athlete who tried to balance his commitments explained why he took a year off from his sport to care for his family: "You can't exercise on Saturday and let that carry you the rest of the week. [Similarly], you can't just visit with your family on Saturday. There has to be almost daily interaction with the family."

Some Christians have been committed to more than their own athletic success. Quarterback Kurt Warner lost his starting position to Mark Bulger during the 2004 NFL season. At halftime of a game in which Bulger had performed poorly, Warner was asked by his coach Mike Martz to start the second half. Warner argued against that plan: "I basically told coach...

if this was the guy that you're going to build your future around, you've got to play him through these things ... It was just something that he'd always done with me." Coach Martz was impressed: "That just doesn't happen in professional sports. But that was genuine. That was the real deal." That is genuine. That is real. That is whole-life Christianity.

Christian coaches can take the lead in encouraging athletes to develop whole-life commitments. When a mother asked high-school coach Biff Poggi how successful he thought that the boys would be in the coming football season, Poggi answered: "Won't really know for twenty years." The mother was puzzled. Biff explained that it would take twenty years to "see what kind of husbands they are. I'll be able to see what kind of fathers they are. I'll see what they're doing in the community." Poggi proclaims to his boys that God weighs their worth with a different set of scales than the sportsworld does.

The Worship of Sport

When nearly 5000 members of the media converge yearly on the Super Bowl, when most high-school boys value athletic achievement over all other achievement, when family calendars bow to the athletic calendar, sports has become an alternate god. As a god, it attempts to meet genuine, God-given needs.

The Need for Transcendence

Former NFL quarterback Gary Cuozzo discussed the emotional impact of performing before packed stadiums:

Several years ago I returned for an old-timers' reunion. I cannot describe the feeling when I walked on that field and felt the sixty-five thousand people surrounding me, heard their noise, anticipated the whistle for the kickoff. I started to quiver. I had goose bumps. I wanted to cry. You must have competed at that level to know what it's like. It is an eerie, otherworldly experience.

This "other-worldly experience" reflects a universal need for transcendence, the need to feel a part of something beyond ourselves. When my wife and I were in college we spent a week at a conference with more than 500 other Christians from other colleges. We were new to the faith and a minority on a campus that was mostly hostile to the faith. Though both of us had been reluctant witnesses, that large conference transformed us. It gave us a greater boldness and confidence in our faith. We now felt a connection to a worldwide movement: *All over the world this gospel is producing fruit and growing, just as it has been doing among you.* (Col. 1:6) Only the worship of God can wholly satisfy our need for transcendence.

The Need for Significance

Writing in his book, *Ball Four,* Jim Bouton explained that as he was coming to the end of his career, he finally realized that no baseball success could ultimately meet his needs:

Somehow my past successes hadn't made me feel secure. There were all these thoughts racing through my mind, fragments of this and that. It was like listening to twelve radio stations at

once. Sometimes I'd get this tightness in my chest and it felt
as if I was buried ten feet underground breathing through
a straw. The illusion was always that it would come with
the next achievement. If I could just find that ultimate
accomplishment, I'd be safe.

But the Apostle Paul explained the achievement that will
ground our lives: *So then, men ought to regard us as servants of*
Christ and as those entrusted with the secret things of God. Now it is
required that those who have been given a trust must prove faithful.
(1 Cor.4:1-3) Whether a person is an athlete or an architect or
an accountant, he will find a secure and lasting significance by
becoming a faithful servant to his heavenly Father.

The Need for Community

The Brooklyn Dodgers won the National League Pennant five
times between 1941 and 1953. But each year lost to the New
York Yankees in the World Series. The phrase "Wait 'til next
year!" became the unofficial team slogan. But in 1955 they finally broke through and won the World Series. Thomas Oliphant,
in his memoir of that season, *Praying for Gil Hodges*, explained
how he, his parents, and his fellow Brooklynites responded:
"The most interesting reaction was that tens of thousands of
people like us simply poured out of their dwellings and hung
around on the streets." Church bells all over the city rang out.
And "everybody looked like us, beaming and laughing.... The
overwhelmingly dominant impression was of mass joy."

Why does winning a championship game produce so much

communal joy? Because in our fragmented communities, the local sports teams have become our communal glue. Formerly, it was religious festivals that bound people together—baptisms, confirmations, marriages, deaths. These events served to bring "the community together to reaffirm its common purpose, common origins, and common beliefs." But what do modern sports fans share in common? Only the welfare of the team. And that union tends to unravel quickly once the championship fades into yesterday's news. It lacks the power to keep races or families or communities working side by side to solve life's problems.

The first century Jew-Gentile conflict was as deep as any racial conflict of our day. But in the early church Jews and Gentiles forged a unity, enabling them to eat, worship, and serve side by side. What was the source of their unity? Christ *is our peace, who has made the two one and has destroyed the barrier; the dividing wall of hostility.* (Eph. 2:14). When we experience this Christ-bred and Christ-fed unity, we proclaim that the worship of God alone will satisfy our longing for community.

The Need for Clarity

We live in a complex world with complex problems. Why have education scores plummeted? Is it the breakdown of the family? A lack of money? Poorly trained teachers? Life's problems can be baffling. But, as sportswriter Leonard Koppett observed, sports share little of that ambiguity. In any championship game, "the hits and errors will be clear, and the heroes and goats will be identified. In sports there are clear rules, boundaries, foul-lines, endlines, goal lines, and referees or umpires to decide by instant decisions or instant replays what really happened." When I play golf I get a definite score. But where is the objective measurement in my job? My home? My relationship with God?

Christians don't have to escape to the comforting clarity of the sportsworld. We have a Lord who provides us with *more and more knowledge and depth of insight, so that [we] may be able to discern what is best.* (Phil. 1:9) And even when the path is unclear, we can confidently say: *Even though I walk through the valley of the shadow of death, I will fear no evil, for you are with me; your rod and your staff, they comfort me.* (Psalms 23:4).

Conclusion

New York Knicks basketball was Richard Lipsky's shelter while his personal life was collapsing. Lipsky explains in his book, *How We Play the Game,* that each home game was like a revival meeting. Madison Square Gardens "became a place of worship, the sports pages of the *New York Post* became holy writ. [The journalists] fed the devotional spirit. Fans read about the dramatic confrontation before entering that night's contest." As the Knicks made a run at the NBA championship, "a warm camaraderie" developed among the fans. During the championship series, when it was questionable whether their injured star, Willis Reed, would play, the fans leaped out of their seats and embraced each other when Reed entered the arena. Lipsky said he experienced "the same feeling he used to get as a kid when the cavalry appeared on the hill to rescue the helpless settlers."

When the Knicks won the championship, it was the emotional peak of Lipsky's life:

> *I was soaking wet. I yelled out the window. My suffering had been redeemed. I felt as if no one could ever understand my feelings. Ever since I had been a 5'1" seventh grader, I had dreamed of being a Knick. I had practiced for hours, six and seven days a week. I was a good player, but I was never going to be a Knick. Yet somehow at that moment I was a Knick. I had given the team and the game of basketball a huge chunk of my emotional life, and I was repaid in this moment of mystical communion.*

I understand Lipsky's emotions. Much of my early emotional life was tied to personal or vicarious athletic achievements. I became trapped in the seductive web of the sportsworld. The hope of sportsworld glory captured my whole being.

As Christians, we must proclaim an even more compelling vision—the vision of serving the King of kings and the Lord of lords. We can begin to counter the athletic dream of fame and money and roaring crowds by proclaiming the infinite difference between earthly and heavenly rewards. An athlete can pursue ephemeral human praise or eternal divine praise:

> *Well done, good and faithful servant! You have been faithful with a few things; I will put you in charge of many things. Come and share your master's happiness! (Matt. 25:23)*

AFTERWORD

"If we parents are the crucial variable in determining whether our kids do time at Duke or Leavenworth, then we can't relax for even a moment."

— Dr. Alvin Rosenfeld, Child Psychiatrist

"Do you not know that in a race all the runners run, but only one gets the prize? Run in such a way as to get the prize."

— 1 Cor. 9:24

One night, while observing an intense basketball game, Scott Sansberry had a revelation. After one of the opposing players committed a "dastardly deed"—a personal foul!—Sansberry bellowed: "Number 52, you bum!"

Though my voice was just one amid a cacophony of 3000, he heard me. Number 52 looked over at me, at this lynch-mob moron who had just screamed at him. He cocked a half-grin. And winked at me. *It's okay, buddy,* that wink said. *I understand.* It was as if I was awakened from a twenty-year sleep. Clouds parting, angels singing, twenty-one-gun salutes, free trips to Disneyland, the whole package. In that single moment, I was gifted with a new perspective, a new understanding of where I had gone wrong, of how easily people could be deluded into creating false adversaries, a me-against-the-bad-guys game that can span an entire existence. Number 52 was not a bum. He was just a guy, playing a game, and he was having a good time doing it.

Like Mr. Sansberry, many of us need a transformed perspective on sports. In a world of hunger and hurricanes, genocide and joblessness, is it a tragedy if your child's coach is inept? Or your daughter wasn't chosen for the first team? Or that a referee called a bogus foul on your son? Many of us parents need to step back, take three deep breaths, and remind ourselves: "This is not the end of my child's life!"

Bruce Svare's father had a healthy perspective on his son's athletics: "I don't remember my father ever saying anything negative to me about my athletic performance, second-guessing a coach, criticizing one of my teammates, grousing about my playing time, chastising an official, or boasting to other parents. He enjoyed the fact that I liked athletics and had some success at it, but he never reveled in it." Oh, that there were more parents who shared Mr. Svare's perspective on their children's sports. This more relaxed view might give a child the space she needs to develop her actual, God-given talents.

Svare observes that we formerly thought that only a "lucky few individuals were born beautiful, brilliant, or athletically gifted...A human being's basic endowment could not be tampered with, before or after birth. It was what you had to work with—or around." Many modern parents think that all children can be superstars if a parent "will take their development very seriously and foster it actively." But our kids don't need us to throw a full-court press on any aspect of their development!

What children do need are parents who have a vision for eternity. That is, parents who are more concerned about helping their children train for God's forever rewards rather than the fleeting rewards of the sportsworld:

> *Everyone who competes in the games goes into strict training.*
> *They do it to get a crown that will not last; but we do it to get*
> *a crown that will last forever. (1 Cor. 9:25-26)*

ABOUT THE AUTHOR

Dr. Bernie Schock is an author (*Parents, Kids, and Sports: Remodeling the Family*), a professor (Biblical Studies at the University of Sioux Falls), a husband (45 years and counting!), a father (3 sons who competed in sports from grade school through college), a volunteer coach (soccer & basketball), a fan (Minnesota Twins & University of Illinois basketball) and an athlete (golf & pickup basketball at the "Y"!). Throughout his adult life he has sought to understand how sports and the sportsworld impact the development of children. This is his second book on that subject.